Eucharistic Celebration
1789-1989

Eucharistic Celebration 1789-1979

Byron D. Stuhlman

THE CHURCH HYMNAL CORPORATION, NEW YORK

Figures 2, 3, 5, 6, and 7 in the Appendix
are reproduced with the permission of
Dell Upton, author of *Holy Things and Profane*
(MIT Press, Cambridge, MA, 1986).

The Church Hymnal Corporation
800 Second Avenue
New York, NY 10017

5   4   3   2   1

Table of Contents

Author's Preface

This work was commissioned by the Church Hymnal Corporation to commemorate the two-hundredth anniversary of the American Book of Common Prayer (1789–1989). It is not a work of original scholarship, but attempts a synthesis of many studies in recent years on various aspects of the topic. The most notable feature of our first American Book of Common Prayer was the fact that the Eucharist in that book was descended in significant ways not from the English Book of Common Prayer, but from the Communion Office of the tiny Episcopal Church of Scotland. This book seeks to trace the historical journey from the adoption of Scottish features in that first American book to the Book of Common Prayer 1979 and then to look toward the future.

It is a fascinating story, and much of it is not widely known. It is one thing to trace the text of the rite. It is a more difficult task to trace how the rite was celebrated, experienced, and understood. We are all—no matter where we locate ourselves in the theological spectrum—heirs of the Oxford Movement, which so transformed our worship that we have forgotten much of our past. There is no recent book that has tried to tell the whole story, and there is much to be learned from that story. Readers of the manuscript for this book have expressed the conviction that the story deserves the attention not only of seminarians, clergy, and scholars, but of Episcopalians in general.

For this reason, the author has added some tools designed to assist the general reader, who may not be conversant with technical theological and liturgical vocabulary—an Appended Note to Chapter 1, an appendix of schematic architectural plans, and a glossary of theological and liturgical terms. The general reader may still find Chapter 1 slow going, but should persevere: that chapter establishes the groundwork for further developments.

The author wishes to acknowledge his gratitude to readers of the manuscript of this book, especially Dr. Carol Doran, Dr. Donald Gerardi, Mr. Raymond Glover, the Rev. Marion Hatchett, the Rev. Joseph Russell, and the Rev. Louis Weil, all of whom offered encouragement and helpful suggestions.

Byron David Stuhlman

The Feast of the Presentation, 1988

AUTHOR'S PREFACE

The Prelude to the American Rite of 1789

When in 1789 the American Episcopal Church adopted its first Book of Common Prayer, the English Book of Common Prayer had already been in use in America for nearly two centuries—since the settlement in Jamestown in 1607. The Prayer Book had undergone a very minor revision in 1604 and a slightly more extensive one in 1662, but the Eucharist most Anglican inhabitants of British North America would have known was for all practical purposes the 1559 Elizabethan revision of the English rite of 1552. The frequency with which the sacrament was celebrated would have varied from age to age and place to place, but it would generally be no less than quarterly and seldom more than monthly.

When the newly achieved independence of the United States made necessary the revision of the Book of Common Prayer after the American Revolution, it might have been expected that the Eucharist would have remained substantially the same as it had been in the English books used in this country for nearly two hundred years, apart from necessary alterations in which political authorities would be remembered in the intercessions. If further changes were to be made, it would seem likely that they would have been latitudinarian in character, given the rationalist temperament of the times. But the eucharistic rite adopted in the Book of Common Prayer of 1789 was substantially different, and de-

1

scended in significant ways not from the English rite of 1552 but from the Scottish rite of 1764 (and earlier Scottish rites).

It will be the purpose of this book to explore how that happened, and then to observe the developments in eucharistic rite, theology, and practice in the Prayer Books of 1892, 1928, and 1979.

There are surprises along the way on this historical journey. We have alluded to the first of them—the adoption of a Scottish Eucharistic Prayer which reassembled the Cranmerian fragments of the 1552 rite in a very non-Cranmerian way. Let us take brief note of some of the others:

- From the days of Queen Elizabeth I, the Church of England has had a eucharistic theology which is at variance with its eucharistic rite.

- The authentic classical Anglican doctrine of the eucharistic presence, consecration, and the eucharistic sacrifice is not—as the Anglo-Catholics from Tractarian times have imagined— rooted in medieval Western Catholicism at all, but rather in a synthesis of the doctrine of the early fathers, Calvin, and the theology implicit in the early Eastern liturgies.

- Calvin's doctrine of the eucharistic presence was common to most English Christians from the time of Elizabeth. "Puritan" is a label normally used for those (Anglican or separatist) who were strict Calvinists in other matters as well. After the Restoration of the monarchy in 1660, nonepiscopalian Puritans no longer conformed to the Church of England and became Congregationalists or Presbyterians. See the Appended Note to this chapter for a further discussion of Calvinism and Puritanism.

- Early Evangelical and Methodist influences led to a heightening, rather than a diminishing, of eucharistic theology, practice, and piety. Puritan and Methodist alike had a higher eucharistic theology than that of the 1552 rite.

- The principal result of the Tractarian Movement was to create a sacramental theology, practice, and piety at variance with both classical Anglican theology and the distinctive American eucharistic rite. In the heat of the controversy generated by the Tractarians, they and their opponents alike carried on their debate in terms of the "Western rite" (read pre- or post-Tridentine Roman Catholicism) rather than in terms of the authentic rite and theology of the American Prayer Book.

- Liturgical Renewal in many ways has led to stripping off the tractarian overlay of more than a century, and returning to the authentic tradition of classical Anglican theology and the Scottish-American rite.

We begin our historical journey by examining briefly the English rite that would have been known to American Anglicans in 1789, the classical eucharistic theology which they would have learned, and the Scottish rite which they so surprisingly adopted.

The English Rite

On Pentecost, 1549, the First Book of Common Prayer replaced the Roman Rite as the liturgy of the Church of England. The outline of this rite is as follows:

The Proclamation of the Word of God

Introit Psalm
　　Lord's Prayer, Collect for Purity during psalm
Kyrie eleison and Gloria in excelsis
Salutation and Collect of the Day

One of two Collects for the King
Epistle
Gospel
Nicene Creed
Sermon or Homily

The Celebration of the Holy Communion

Exhortation
Offertory Sentences
  Offering of money in the poor men's box
  movement of communicants into choir
  preparation of bread and wine and placement on table
Eucharistic Prayer
  Salutation, Sursum Corda, Preface, Sanctus/Benedictus
  Intercessions (Prayer for the Whole State of Christ's
    Church)
  Post-Sanctus and Invocation (hanc igitur, quam oblationem)
  Institution Narrative (qui pridie)
    manual acts: taking bread and cup
    elevation prohibited
  Memorial or anamnesis (unde et memores)
  Prayer for acceptance (supra quae, supplices te, nobis
    quoque)
  Doxology
Lord's Prayer
Peace
Anthem "Christ our Paschal Lamb"
Invitation, Confession, Absolution, Comfortable Words
Prayer of Humble Access
Fraction and Communion with Agnus Dei
Postcommunion sentence and collect
Blessing

Reference to this outline (in which initial Latin words for comparable parts of the Roman Canon are given) will reveal that the Eucharist in this rite was in many respects a skillful English rendition of the Latin service it replaced. It maintained the traditional shape of that rite but removed much of the overlay of ceremonial accretion and private prayers of the celebrant which had accumulated during the Middle Ages. It was a liturgy designed to emphasize *continuity* in worship. Eucharistic vestments were retained and a restrained use of ceremonial and music was continued. The noteworthy feature of the rite was the provision of a full eucharistic prayer loosely based on the Roman Canon but revised to avoid two doctrines repudiated at the Reformation:

1. the Eucharist as a propitiatory sacrifice;

2. transubstantiation and the corporal presence of Christ's physical body and blood under the forms of bread and wine.

To many in later ages, this eucharistic rite has seemed a liturgical masterpiece; in its day, however, it satisfied neither the conservatives (who nonetheless read into it the two doctrines it was designed to repudiate) nor the radical reformers (who disliked its apparent continuity with the traditional rite).

Consequently, a revised Book of Common Prayer went into use on All Saints' Day, 1552 (its use proved short-lived: Mary Tudor restored the Roman rite on her accession in 1553). The eucharistic liturgy of this book was explicitly designed to emphasize *discontinuity* with the traditional rite and to make it impossible to read the repudiated doctrines into it. In fact, the texts and gestures cited by the conservatives in reading these doctrines into the 1549 service were deleted or altered. The revisers wished to make their repudiation of transubstantiation and of the doctrine of the Eucharist as a propitiatory sacrifice unmistakable. W. Jardine Grisbrooke summarizes the results in this way:[1]

Briefly, to Cranmer whatever presence of the Body and Blood of our Lord there may be in the Lord's Supper, it is in no wise *specifically* connected with the bread and wine therein taken, distributed, and consumed; and whatever there may be of sacrifice in the rite is in no way connected either with the bread and wine, or with the Body and Blood of our Lord.

These are the doctrines which the Communion Service of the Book of Common Prayer was intended to embody and express, and which it does embody and express very successfully.

The resulting outline may be seen in the following table:

The Proclamation of the Word of God

Lord's Prayer and Collect for Purity
Decalogue with Kyrie as response
Collect of the Day (no salutation)
One of two Collects for the King
Epistle
Gospel
Nicene Creed
Sermon or Homily
Offertory Sentences and Collection of offerings (alms)
Prayer for the Whole State of Christ's Church Militant here in earth

The Celebration of the Holy Communion

Exhortation
Invitation, Confession, Absolution, Comfortable Words
Sursum Corda, Preface, and Sanctus (no Salutation or Benedictus)

CHAPTER ONE:

Prayer of Humble Access
1549 post-Sanctus and Institution Narrative (no manual acts)
Communion
Lord's Prayer
Prayer of Oblation or 1549 Postcommunion Prayer
Gloria in excelsis
Blessing

In the Proclamation of the Word of God (to use the language of the 1979 Book of Common Prayer), note that the introit psalm has been deleted, the Kyrie eleison replaced Geneva fashion by the Decalogue with the Kyrie as a response, and the Gloria in excelsis transposed to the end of the service. In addition, the intercessions (with prayer for the departed and commemoration of the saints removed) have been lifted out of the eucharistic prayer to become, with the collection of alms which precede them, part of the Ante-Communion.

It is, however, the Celebration of the Holy Communion that has been most drastically altered. There is no rubrical provision for the preparation of the bread and wine. The celebration begins with the exhortation and the penitential order (invitation, confession, absolution, and comfortable words). The eucharistic prayer is broken up into parts. The Sursum Corda, preface, and Sanctus (without the Benedictus qui venit) follow the exhortation and then the Prayer of Humble Access is said. This is followed by the institution narrative, introduced by the text which follows the intercessions in 1549, but with the invocation of the Spirit changed into a prayer for fruitful communion. The act of Communion itself follows. The traditional 1549 words of administration were: "The Body of our Lord Jesus Christ which was given for thee preserve thy body and soul unto everlasting life. The Blood of our Lord Jesus Christ which was shed for thee preserve thy body and soul unto everlasting life." In 1552 they were replaced by a new set: "Take and eat this in remembrance that Christ died for thee, and feed on him in thy heart by faith with thanksgiving. Drink this in remembrance that Christ's blood was shed for thee, and be thankful."

The anamnesis or memorial of Christ's sacrifice (which had followed the institution narrative in the eucharistic prayer in 1549) is deleted, and the Lord's Prayer follows Communion, with the final paragraph of the 1549 eucharistic prayer (whose major theme is self-oblation) being given as an alternative postcommunion prayer. The anthem "Christ our Paschal Lamb" and the Agnus Dei are deleted. The most remarkable feature of the rite was the explicit verbal dissociation of Christ's presence with the bread and wine, found in the Black Rubric at the end of the service denying any "real or essential presence" of "Christ's natural flesh and blood." This rubric was not, in fact, the work of the revisers, but was inserted into the text after it had gone to the printers by order of the Council.

The rubrics of the service now replaced the traditional eucharistic vestments with the cassock and surplice. References to the altar were changed to read "table," and the table was moved into the midst of the chancel or the nave, placed lengthwise, with the celebrant on one side and the communicants gathered round. While music was prepared for the 1549 rite by John Merbecke, it was not adapted to the 1552 rite, and the rite was generally celebrated without music (except for the metrical psalms that were now sometimes sung before and after services). Ceremonial was also pruned. The 1549 Book had indicated the use of the sign of the cross in the eucharistic prayer (at the invocation), had provided manual acts at the institution narrative (taking the bread and the wine into the hands—though elevation was explicitly forbidden), and had directed that the breads were to be broken before they were distributed. All this disappeared in the 1552 rite.

This rite is the low-water mark of Anglican eucharistic doctrine. Historically, Anglican eucharistic doctrine is most closely akin to that of the Swiss reformers, but so negative an expression of the eucharistic presence as we find in this rite is not characteristic of Calvin. Indeed, the labels "Zwinglian" and "Calvinist" can be misleading, for the doctrine of these reformers went through several stages of development in the heat of controversy, and in Anglican writing the labels are often applied to only the minimalist expression of their doctrine. Cranmer himself was under intense pressure from the more radical reformers in England when he drafted the 1552 Book, and it is not certain that the rite found there is the liturgical expression that he would prefer of his own doctrine, though he defended the rite and was certainly at this time in accord with the Swiss reformers in his belief. It has proved difficult if not impossible to define Cranmer's own belief in this matter with precision, and in the end the relevant question is how the Church of England came to understand the rite, not what Cranmer intended.

In 1559 the Elizabethan Prayer Book replaced the Roman Rite that had been restored under Mary Tudor. Its eucharistic liturgy is basically that of 1552, with the Black Rubric deleted, the 1549 words of administration prefaced to those of 1552, and an ornaments rubric that stipulated (largely without success) the use of the traditional eucharistic vestments. These changes, while relatively minor, are significant: the 1552 service is to be interpreted in a more traditional manner than its text in and of itself would warrant. In 1562, the 42 articles drafted in 1553 were revised and adopted as the 39 Articles. Significant changes were made in the articles which related to the Eucharist. These articles declare that Christ's body and blood "are given, taken, and received in the supper only after an heavenly and spiritual manner." While this article in its formulation sounds negative, study of its interpretation at the time indicates that it was intended to defend a true presence of Christ in the sacrament, but one that was spiritual rather than corporal or physical. It represents, then, a heightening of sacramental doctrine. The Prayer Book was revised again after the accession of James VI and I. This revision did not alter the eucharistic rite, but did include (at the urging of the Puritans) a new section of the catechism dealing with the sacraments. Here the doctrine of Christ's presence is put in positive terms: "the Body and Blood of Christ are verily and indeed taken and received by the faithful in the Lord's Supper." During the reign of James and of his son Charles I the high-church school gradually gained ascendancy and adopted a more ceremonial form of worship. In particular, the preference for an altar-wise placement of the communion table came to prevail and was enforced by canon. Archbishop Laud also insisted that the altar be railed—an innovation which has taken such firm root that we tend to forget that it was a highly controversial imposition at the time, and was considered theologically significant.

During the Commonwealth the use of the Book of Common Prayer was prohibited. When Charles II was restored to the throne, a new revision of the Prayer Book was prepared and issued in 1662 (the edition still in force in England). Negotiations to prepare this revision were held with both Presbyterians and Anglicans represented. Both groups came with their own agenda: Presbyterians desiring a less liturgical and ceremonious rite, Anglicans preferring a rite like that of 1549 or the abortive liturgy of 1637 prepared for the Church of Scotland. The outcome was something of a stalemate: the changes to the 1604 rite adopted were, in fact, mostly agreeable to both Presbyterians and Anglicans, although the book as a whole was unsatisfactory to Presbyterians, who left the Church of England at this time. These changes included rubrics requiring manual acts (including a fraction) during the institution narrative and the inclusion of the title "The Prayer of Consecration" in the rubric introducing the eucharistic prayer. The Laudians also succeeded in retaining the ornaments rubric (eucharistic vestments did not in fact come back into use, although copes were not uncommon), in restoring a rubric regulating the preparation of the bread and wine, and in retaining the traditional placement of the altar. Rubrics also provided for supplementary consecration if necessary and for the reverent consumption of consecrated elements remaining after communion. A modified form of the Black Rubric was restored; it denied, however, the "corporal," not the "real or essential" presence of Christ in the sacrament.

Classical Anglican Eucharistic Theology

Classical Anglican Eucharistic theology developed its own distinctive doctrines of the Eucharistic Presence, Consecration, and the Eucharistic Sacrifice. In all three cases, the doctrinal development can be traced in the appeal of Anglican theologians and apologists to the primitive church. In all three cases, the classical forms of the doctrines may be *read into* the English rite after 1552, but are not really consistent with it. In other words, the Church of England began to develop a eucharistic theology which was at variance with, though not in absolute contradiction to, its eucharistic liturgy. That is not to say that Anglican theologians abandoned their respect for Swiss Reformed—especially Calvinist—theology. In their doctrine of the Eucharistic Presence and the related doctrine of consecration, Calvin and their reading of the Eastern fathers and Eastern liturgical texts reinforced each other in large part.

The doctrine of Christ's Eucharistic Presence posed a problem at the Reformation, in large part because the philosophical and metaphysical language of the day provided no adequate means for the reformers to formulate their religious convictions. The reformers were unanimous in rejecting the doctrine of transubstantiation because, as the 39 Articles declare, it overthrows the nature of a sacrament, denying the reality of the outward and visible sign in order to affirm the reality of what the sign signifies. The Lutheran solution, which is generally labeled "consubstantiation," although Lutherans have never been comfortable with the label, affirms that the sacrament conveys the substance of the body and blood of Christ along with the substance of the bread and wine, and was rejected by other reformers as a solution because (in the words of the Black Rubric) "as concerning the natural body and blood of our savior Christ, they are in heaven and not here. For it is against the truth of Christ's natural body, to be in more places than in one, at one time." This argument, advanced by both Zwingli and Calvin, was accepted by Anglican reformers as well.

The term "real presence" is an ambiguous one which bedevils discussion of the doctrine of Christ's presence, because of the different ways in which the word "real" is understood. Early reformers generally used the word in a narrow philosophical sense, as we see in the 1662 revision of the Black Rubric where it was replaced with "corporal." In the broader sense of "true," it expressed a doctrine which most of the Reformers wanted to affirm. Swiss theologians who followed Calvin strove earnestly to guard against an expression of eucharistic doctrine which seemed to reduce Christ's presence to a merely subjective reality dependent on the faith of the communicant. After the heat of the early eucharistic controversies in the first years of the English Reformations, Puritans and high Anglicans alike tended to avoid Zwinglian minimalism, and hold a Calvinist doctrine of the eucharistic presence.

The points at issue were succinctly set forth by William Nicholson, Restoration Bishop of Gloucester:[2]

CHAPTER ONE:

Christ is said to be present in four manner of ways:—

1. Divinely, as God, and so He is present in all places. *Whither shall I fly from Thy presence? I, the Lord, fill heaven and earth.*

2. Spiritually, and so He is present in the hearts of true believers. *Christ dwells in our hearts by faith.*

3. Sacramentally, and so is He present in the Sacrament, because He hath ordained the Sacrament to represent and communicate Christ's death unto us. *The cup of blessing which we bless, is it not the communion of the blood of Christ, etc.?*

4. Corporally; so present in Judaea in the days of His flesh.

And as the word "presence," so the word "really," is diversely taken; for sometimes,

1. It is opposed to that which is feigned, and is but imaginary, and imports as much as "truly."

2. It is opposed to that which is merely figurative, and barely representative, and imports as much as "effectually."

3. It is opposed to that which is spiritual, and imports as much as "corporally" or "bodily."

We then believe Christ to be present in the Eucharist Divinely after a special manner, Spiritually in the hearts of the communicants, Sacramentally or relatively in the elements. And this presence of His is real, in the two former acceptions of "real"; but not in the last, for He is truly and effectually there present, though not corporally, bodily, carnally, locally.

In the first years after the Reformation, Anglicans tended to avoid the term "real presence" because of its ambiguity and to articulate their belief in other ways. The word "mystery" or "mysteries" in the eucharistic rite of the Book of Common Prayer (in all editions) is perhaps one of these ways. Calvin used this expression to express the effectual reality of communion with Christ in the sacrament. Typically, later writers will speak of Christ's presence as a mystery, whose reality is secured by the words of Christ, but whose manner cannot be defined. John Cosin writes,[3]

> As to the manner of the presence of the Body and Blood of Our Lord in the Blessed Sacrament, we that are Protestant and Reformed according to the ancient Catholic Church do not search into the manner of it with perplexing inquiries; but after the example of the primitive and purest Church of Christ, we leave it to the power and wisdom of Our Lord, yielding a full and unfeigned assent to His words.

A second way of approaching the reality of the eucharistic presence is to speak of "participation," one way of rendering the word "communion." Richard Hooker sets out the following as the most satisfactory way of interpreting the words, "This is my Body:"[4]

> this hallowed food, through concurrence of divine power, is in verity and truth unto faithful receivers instrumentally a cause of that mystical participation, whereby, as I make Myself wholly theirs, so I give them in hand an actual possession of all such saving grace as my sacrificed Body can yield, and as their souls do presently need, this is to them and in them My Body.

This view has been characterized as "dynamic or instrumental symbolism" or "dynamic receptionism." It articulates a high view of the sacrament carefully constructed within the framework of Calvinist doctrine. Louis Weil summarizes Hooker's achievement in this way:[5]

This statement offers a summary of the primary affirmations which Anglicanism has taught about the Eucharist:

1. that the physical elements remain material food;

2. that the elements are sanctified by divine power;

3. that the elements are instruments of the grace offered to mankind through the sacrifice of Christ;

4. that those who receive the elements in faith have access in them to this gift of saving grace.

Much is said, but also much is left undefined. The balance in Hooker's definition may easily be overthrown by a greater emphasis on one point or another. The reference to "faithful receivers," for example, can easily become a basis for a receptionist view if it is not held in tension with a belief that the "hallowed food" is "instrumentally a cause" of Christ's presence.

In the eighteenth century and early nineteenth, this "dynamic receptionism" would probably be the most common doctrine of the eucharistic presence among American Anglicans. As it was set forth by Daniel Waterland, it was the doctrine of such high-churchmen as Samuel Johnson and John Henry Hobart.

The later form of the essentially Calvinist doctrine articulated by Hooker represents a somewhat higher view of the eucharistic presence, placing the emphasis on Christ's presence and omitting faithful reception from the terms of the definition, and is generally known as "dynamic virtualism." Its name comes from its assertion that the Holy Spirit renders the Body and Blood of Christ present not in substance, but in power or "virtue." John Johnson, rector of Cranbrook in Kent, is the classic spokesman for this doctrine:[6]

1. The Body and Blood in the Sacrament are the Bread and Wine.

2. The Body and Blood in the Sacrament, or the Consecrated Bread and Wine, are Types of the Natural Body and Blood of Christ.

3. But they are not such cold and imperfect Types as those before and under the Law.

4. Nay, they are the very Body and Blood, tho' not in Substance, yet in Spirit, Power, and Effect.

This was the view that the mature Samuel Seabury was to espouse, and it had other American advocates as well, particularly among those influenced by the Scottish Episcopalians. John Henry Hobart originally held this view, but eventually adopted a more receptionist doctrine, as we have noted above.

With this, we move onto the next doctrinal issue, the question of how the presence of Christ is effected in the sacrament, or how the bread and wine become instruments by which the communicant participates in the Body and Blood of Christ. This is the doctrine of Consecration. Occasionally, consecration is said to be achieved by the action of Christ. Bishop George Bull, citing Justin and Irenaeus, puts the doctrine in this way:[7]

> by or upon the sacerdotal benediction, the Spirit of Christ, or a divine virtue of Christ descends upon the elements, and accompanies them to all faithful communicants, and . . . therefore they are said to be and are the Body and Blood of Christ; the same divinity which is hypostatically united to the Body of Christ in heaven, being virtually united to the elements of Bread and Wine upon earth. Which also seems to be the meaning of all the ancient liturgies, in which it is prayed, "that God would send down His Spirit upon the bread and wine in the Eucharist."

Bull has phrased the doctrine in this way to accommodate it to the Prayer of Consecration as found in the English rite, whose core is the recital of the institution narrative, but the ancient texts he cites really fit more easily in a eucharistic prayer which includes an invocation of the Spirit, which disappeared from the English rite in 1552. His doctrine would seem to approach the Lutheran doctrine which Anglicans generally rejected, although he gives it a virtualist twist, and it was not common—at least in this form. A less precise form of this doctrine simply holds that consecration is effected by the words of Christ spoken by the celebrant. The logic of the English "prayer of consecration" after 1552 leads to this conclusion, since there is no invocation of the Spirit.

The more usual doctrine of consecration, however, was that of Calvin and of the Eastern Church, that it was effected by the invocation of the Spirit. This is the Puritan doctrine as found in the Westminster Directory, which regulated worship in England during the Commonwealth. It also is the reason that Anglicans came to prefer the 1549 rite with its explicit invocation of the Holy Spirit upon the elements or the abortive Scottish liturgy of 1637 with its similar invocation to the rites of the English Prayer Books of 1552 and subsequently. John Johnson again sets forth the classic expression of this doctrine, moving beyond Calvin and basing his theology on the eucharistic prayers of the Eastern Church:[8]

> the Holy Ghost was, by the Vote of Antiquity, the principal immediate Cause of the Bread and Wine's becoming the Body and Blood. . . .
>
> the Subordinate or Mediate Cause of it is, 1. The Reciting of the Words of Institution. 2. The Oblation of the Symbols. 3. The Prayer of Invocation. All these did, in the ancient Liturgies, immediately follow each other, in the order that I have mentioned them; and each of them was believed to contribute toward the Consecration of the Elements into the Body and Blood.

This is an accurate theology of the Byzantine Rite. It does not, however, fit either the English rites since 1552 or even the 1549 rite or the Scottish rite of 1637. As W. Jardine Grisbrooke notes,[9] "Johnson himself, it is true, reconciled his teaching with the liturgy of 1662, but nowhere does he vouchsafe an answer to the pertinent query how he did so." With Johnson, we have reached a development in Anglican eucharistic theology which will result in the Scottish eucharistic rite of 1764 and the American Prayer Book of 1789.

For those who held a receptionist doctrine of the eucharistic presence, the function of the consecration needs to be put somewhat differently. From this standpoint, the consecration sets the elements apart for the purpose of communion, but Christ becomes present in the elements at the time of reception rather than at the time of consecration, or is present to the communicants at the time of reception.

We turn now to the doctrine of the Eucharistic Sacrifice. The Anglican objection to the medieval doctrine as they understood it is found in the 39 Articles: "The Offering of Christ once made is that perfect redemption, propitiation, and satisfaction, for all the sins of the whole world, both original and actual; and there is none other satisfaction for sin, but that alone. Wherefore the sacrifices of Masses, in which it was commonly said, that the Priest did offer Christ for the quick and the dead, to have remission of pain or guilt, were blasphemous fables, and dangerous deceits." It can be seen here that what the Reformers sought to avoid was the idea of a separate propitiatory significance for the eucharistic oblation—an offering of Christ on the part of the celebrant at the Eucharist. The fact that the bread and wine are offered to God in the Roman Canon after the institution narrative, which was thought to effect their consecration as the Body and Blood of Christ, is what gave rise to the doctrine that the Reformers sought to avoid. The section of the Anglican eucharistic prayer which follows the Sanctus (or the Prayer of Humble Access) sets forth the Reformation doctrine in no uncertain terms:

> [Christ] made there, by his one oblation of himself once offered, a full, perfect, and sufficient sacrifice, oblation, and satisfaction, for the sins of the whole world. . . .

The question of in what sense the Eucharist might be said to be a sacrifice became an ongoing controversy. What is known as the Prayer of Oblation in Cranmer's rites and their derivatives (essentially a prayer of self-oblation on the part of the communicants once the anamnesis or memorial of Christ's sacrifice was deleted in 1552) uses the word "sacrifice" three times:

> we earnestly desire thy fatherly goodness mercifully to accept this our sacrifice of praise and thanksgiving . . . .

> here we offer and present unto thee, O Lord, ourselves, our souls and bodies, to be a reasonable, holy, and living sacrifice unto thee . . . .

> although we are unworthy, through our manifold sins, to offer unto thee any sacrifice, yet we beseech thee to accept this our bounden duty and service, not weighing our merits, but pardoning our offenses . . . .

The Eucharist itself is said to be "a perpetual memory of his precious death" [rites derivative of the 1637 Scottish liturgy will add, "and sacrifice"] "until his coming again." Luther intensely disliked the word "oblation" when used to refer to the bread and wine, for he believed that it was suggestive of the medieval doctrine which he wished to avoid. Out of the same concern the English rite from the beginning has avoided language which suggests that the bread and wine are offered in the Eucharist.

The Reformation dilemma was how to articulate the efficacy of the sacrament without ascribing to it the virtue which properly belongs to Christ's Sacrifice. Puritans tended to avoid the language of sacrifice altogether. John Bramhall, appointed Archbishop of Armagh at the Restoration, perhaps sets out the positive thrust of Anglican teaching most articulately:[10]

> We acknowledge an Eucharistical Sacrifice of praise and thanksgiving; a commemorative Sacrifice or a memorial of the Sacrifice of the cross; a representative Sacrifice, or a representation of the Passion of Christ before the eyes of his heavenly Father; an impetrative Sacrifice, or an impetration of the fruits and benefit of His Passion by way of real prayer; and lastly, an applicative Sacrifice, or an application of his merits unto our souls.

What he denies is a "suppletory Sacrifice, to supply the defects of the Sacrifice of the Cross." This is as high a doctrine of the Eucharistic Sacrifice as can generally be found among Anglicans of the period.

We turn, in conclusion, to several issues related to the doctrine of the Eucharistic Sacrifice: 1. How is the relation between the sacrifice of Christ and the Eucharist articulated? 2. For whom is the Eucharist efficacious? 3. How does the doctrine of the Eucharistic Sacrifice find expression in the words and actions of the eucharistic liturgy?

1. The Eucharist is understood as a memorial or representation of Christ's sacrifice (what is meant in contemporary theological language by "anamnesis"). The Elizabethan Bishop of Salisbury, John Jewel, puts it in this way:[11]

> This sacrifice is revived, and freshly laid out before our eyes in the ministration of the holy mysteries.

CHAPTER ONE:

We offer up Christ, that is to say, an example, a commemoration, a remembrance of the death of Christ.

The ministration of the Holy Communion is sometimes of the ancient fathers called an "unbloody sacrifice," not in respect to any corporal or fleshy presence . . . but for that it representeth and reporteth unto our minds that one and everlasting sacrifice that Christ made in His body upon the cross . . . .

Jeremy Taylor, Restoration Bishop of Down, Connor, and Dromore, is considered by W. Jardine Grisbrooke the first to elaborate the Christology of Hebrews to develop the idea of Christ as a high priest after the order of Melchisedek pleading or offering the sacrifice in the heavenly sanctuary as the celebrant pleads or offers it in the Church's Eucharist[12]—a doctrine that finds visual expression in the frontispiece to the 1720 edition of Charles Wheatly's *Rational Illustration,* where above the priest ministering at the altar in the church Christ is seen in a cloud making the same offering at the altar in the heavenly sanctuary.

John Johnson also articulates this idea very well:[13]

[Christ] did, as a Priest, offer his Body and Blood, in the Eucharist, under the pledges of Bread and Wine; that He was afterwards slain as a Sacrifice on the Cross. . . . He finish'd the Sacrifice of Himself by entering as a High-Priest into Heaven, the true Holy of Holies, and He gives life to our Sacrifice, by always appearing there in the Presence of God for us.

2. Calvinist doctrine (as set forth by Anglican and Puritan alike) speaks of the efficacious nature of the Eucharist by declaring that Christ "seals" the benefits of his death on the cross to us in the reception of Communion. High Anglicans will go beyond this, to label the Eucharist as an "impetrative and applicative" sacrifice, as we have seen above. Eventually, some will come to the conclusion that in this sense it is propitiatory—a doctrine which earlier reformers were concerned to deny. Herbert Thorndike, writes:[14]

> it cannot be denied that the Sacrament of the Eucharist, inasmuch as it is the same Sacrifice of Christ upon the Cross (as that which representeth is truly said to be the thing which it representeth) is also both propitiatory and impetative by virtue of the consecration, whereby it becometh the Sacrifice of Christ upon the Cross.

The question remains, however, for whom is it efficacious? If the answer is that it is efficacious for the faithful communicant, this is akin to the Calvinist doctrine of the sacrament as "sealing" the benefits of the cross to recipients. However, if it is efficacious for others as well, if we can be said to "offer the Eucharist" for others, then we are back to the doctrine which Luther strove mightily to deny and which the 39 Articles repudiate. For John Johnson, who based his eucharistic doctrine on the classic Eastern liturgies which followed the invocation in the eucharistic prayer with intercessions, the Eucharist might also be said to be offered for others of the living besides the communicants, but not for the dead. William Forbes, first Bishop of Edinburgh after the Reformation and a man of irenic temperament and ecumenical sympathies, takes the argument to its logical conclusion, writing that the Eucharist is not only a sacrifice of thanksgiving, "but also propitiatory in a sound sense, and is profitable to very many not only of the living but also of the dead."[15] While this might appear in direct contradiction to the doctrine of the 39 Articles, Kenneth Stevenson comments:[16]

> Forbes saw that the term "propitiatory," which was to be used at Trent, did not mean repeating Calvary, but was a way of describing the Eucharist in dynamic terms.

3. It is readily apparent that the full classical doctrine of the eucharistic sacrifice did not easily find expression in the 1552 rite and its derivatives. We have already noted the three occurrences of the word sacrifice in the prayer of oblation which serves as an alternative postcommunion prayer in this rite and the designation of the Eucharist as a "perpetual memory" in the opening portion of the eucharistic prayer. As Anglicans came to study the eucharistic liturgies of the Eastern churches, however, they came to feel acutely the lack of an oblation of the elements after the institution narrative. This lack remains to this day in the English rite (even in the full eucharistic prayers of the Alternative Services Book). It was remedied only in the liturgy of the Scottish Episcopal Church, to which we shall turn next, and in the rite of the American church which derives from it. In both of these churches, the anamnesis after the institution narrative where the gifts are offered has been explicitly labeled "The Oblation" in the margin.

There is evidence, however, that some celebrants of the English rite recited the prayer of oblation (which is really a prayer of self-oblation) immediately after the institution narrative as a way of providing a more adequate eucharistic prayer. Others, like Lancelot Andrewes, addressed the problem by privately reciting a prayer drawn from the Eastern rites after the institution narrative.

In the Prayer for the Whole State of Christ's Church, some came to interpret the petition for the acceptance of our "alms and oblations" as referring to the bread and wine in the word "oblations," but it is clear that "oblations" as well as "alms" in this context was originally meant to refer to offerings of money.

In regard to the actions required by the rubrics, the 1552, 1559, and 1604 rites also lacked expression of the classical doctrine of the oblation of the bread and wine as an aspect of the eucharistic sacrifice. The restoration of the rubric regarding the preparation of bread and wine and directing the celebrant to place them on the altar after the presentation of the alms in the 1662

Book was considered significant in this regard. The Scottish rites of 1637 and 1764 further directed the celebrant to "offer up" the bread and wine at this point (as did the 1928 edition of the American Book) and this action was sometimes referred to as the "lesser oblation." In recent years an act of oblation at this point in the liturgy has come under criticism (it is a Western tradition, rather than one grounded in Eastern liturgies, and to "take" the bread and wine is not the same thing as to "offer" them). It is noteworthy that the direction to "offer" the bread and wine at this point did not occur in the liturgies of the English nonjurors or in that of Thomas Rattray—liturgies which were directly based on the Eastern rites. Interestingly enough, the Presbyterian rites of the Scottish church made the bringing in of the bread and wine and their placement on the table an action of some solemnity, though they certainly gave no oblatory significance to it.

The fraction itself was given sacrificial interpretation by such diverse theologians as Cranmer's conservative opponent Stephen Gardiner, who read into this action the doctrine of sacrifice that Cranmer had been at pains to repudiate; Lancelot Andrewes, representative of early Anglican high-church views; and the Presbyterians, who made both the breaking of bread and the pouring of the wine significant actions in their rite, making them an acted memorial of Christ's Passion. The 1549 rite required that bread be broken before distribution; no subsequent Prayer Book (not even the Scottish rite of 1637) gave rubrical direction for the fraction until it was restored (during the institution narrative) in the rite of 1662. This is not to say, however, that the bread was not broken: since leavened bread was used, it must necessarily have been broken before distribution. It should be noted that this sacrificial interpretation of the breaking of the bread (articulated in its different ways by both high Anglican and Puritan authors)

CHAPTER ONE:

is not characteristic of the traditional rites such as the Eastern liturgies which proved so attractive to high Anglicans.

A final gesture of some significance is the elevation of the bread and wine in offering during the eucharistic prayer. The significant elevation in the medieval rite had been that during the institution narrative, whose purpose was to offer the consecrated species to worshipers for adoration. But that was not the original significance of the gesture of lifting up the bread and wine: this gesture is in origin one of offering. The Scottish rubric directs that the gifts be "offered *up*" when placed on the table: the gesture is implicit in this rubric. More significant is the custom of raising the gifts in offering during the oblatory prayer after the institution narrative. In the text of Cranmer's 1549 Prayer of Memorial or Oblation, which comes after the narrative, mention is made of the "holy gifts." On the basis of Eastern liturgies, the words "WHICH WE NOW OFFER UNTO THEE" (in upper-case letters) were added to this text by Scots in the eighteenth century, an addition which became official with the rite of 1764. Although no rubric directs the lifting up of the bread and wine at this point, there is evidence that this action was customary—another of the customs derived from the Anglican study of Eastern rites.

Eucharistic theology—the doctrine of the eucharistic presence as well as that of the eucharistic sacrifice—also found expression in the architecture and ceremonial of the rite, and it is to these that we now turn.

The Architectural and Ceremonial Setting of the Eucharist

The architectural setting of worship and the forms of ceremony that worshipers use within this context also reveal much about the theology of the rite.[17] At the time of the Reformation, the use that churches made of the buildings which they inherited and the architectural arrangements they devised for their new buildings were significant signs of the tenor of their theology. So was the kind of behavior expected within the church building—the ceremonial of the people at worship. The rubrics of the Book of Common Prayer give us some clues about these matters, but it is to ecclesiastical legislation and custom and the controversial writings of the period that we must turn if we want to get an accurate view of what worship looked like and felt like in the post-Reformation Church of England and what people thought these factors meant. It is important to make the effort to explore this, because in many ways the architectural setting of Anglican worship and its ceremonial style has changed far more radically over the centuries than have the texts of the Book of Common Prayer. It was also the architectural setting and ceremonial style which most clearly distinguished the Church of England from the reformed churches on the Continent (and in Scotland) whose theology often seems so similar, even as regards the sacraments.

At the time of the Reformation, most churches in England and on the continent were "two-room" spaces. In many reformed churches, buildings were adapted by closing off chancels and using the nave for the liturgy of both word and sacrament. If the liturgy of the word predominated, the pulpit would be the focal point of the space, with a table or a bowl brought in when needed for Communion or Baptism.

English use of the buildings which they inherited was different (although the more extreme Puritans favored the continental usage and followed it when they broke away from the Church of England). To follow more easily the discussion of architecture in the English church, the reader should refer to the schematic architectural plans in the appendix of this book. According to the rubrics of the 1549 rite, the people were seated in the nave for the Proclamation of the Word of God; communicants moved into the chancel at the offertory for the Celebration of the Holy Communion, making their offerings as they came forward. The rubric does not explicitly require this movement of the people in the subsequent editions of the Prayer Book, but in fact communicants generally continued the practice—coming either at the offertory or at the Invitation which introduces the confession. In fact, the bidding to "draw near" in that text may have served in lieu of the rubric.

Chancels, then, were not used in parish churches as places to seat the choristers, but as a place where communicants gathered. As such, it was partitioned off by screens. Elizabeth's Order of 1561 requires this. The old rood was taken down and replaced by the royal arms, but the chancel screen stayed. Indeed, if it had been taken down, it was to be rebuilt. This partitioning provided a space where communicants would not be distracted.

The 1549 Book directs no change in the traditional place of the altar, which customarily was against the east wall of the chancel, but in 1552 the rubric directs that the "table" (as it is now called) be placed "in the body of the church, or in the chancel" at the time of Communion. The rubric is vague, but when the 1559 edition of the rite went into use, Elizabeth determined by her Order of 1561 that the table was to stand in the traditional place except at the time of Communion, when it was moved to the midst of the choir. (The position in the nave was intended as an alternative when the chancel was too small for the communicants to gather in.) In the chancel, seating and forms for kneeling were provided for communicants, and the choir stalls—if there had been such—could also be used for this purpose. Communion itself was administered to people where they had been kneeling for this part of the service. These provisions worked well if the numbers of communicants were not too great. But often the chancel would be crowded, and some communicants might be required to remain in the nave. With crowding, administering Communion in this way became difficult, and it might be equally difficult to administer it to those in box pews in the nave.

The inconvenience of moving the table often led to leaving it in one place, and its placement in the midst of the choir or the nave often led people to treat it casually as just another piece of furniture. For this reason, in the early years of the seventeenth century, the high church party then in the ascendancy began to insist that the table remain always against the east wall and that it be railed to protect it from profanation. The rail also provided a more convenient way of administering Communion to people—so much so, that people are often surprised that rails were not usual at the reformation and that their use for Communion was a new practice. The Puritans, and even moderate churchmen, fiercely protested this new policy. At the Restoration, however, the policy was maintained, and by the end of the century came to seem proper to all schools of churchmen, though there remained places where the old way persisted into the Victorian era.

For a while, two-room churches were built in what has been called the "Gothic survival" style (a term indicating the survival of Gothic elements in the design of churches, even after other styles of architecture had become predominant), but churches built in the seventeenth century began to be built as one-room spaces: a chancel would still be provided at the front for the altar table with space around its rails for communicants, but it would be a unified space, and would not necessarily require the movement of communicants to the chancel at the offertory, since all could hear and see the minister at the altar when the interior of the church was organized in this way. Reading desk and pulpit, of which we will speak later, would be along the side of the church (or one side, when they were combined in one unit), or even above or in front of the altar. Churches of this type are sometimes called "auditory churches," a name devised by Christopher Wren because they were designed with the requirements that people *hear* and see in mind.

By the Royal Order of 1561 the table was not to be left bare, but to be covered with an appropriate cloth (often this is referred to as a "carpet") which would be made of comely and often costly material and hang down to the floor on all sides. At Communion, it would also be covered by a fair linen. When the tables were placed permanently in the traditional position for the altar, they were usually set off by a wood or stone reredos or a tapestry hanging. A frequent form for the reredos was a board with the Decalogue, to the sides of which were often the Apostles' Creed and the Lord's Prayer. Communion vessels and an alms basin in precious metals would be provided for the altar, and a cushion for the altar book. On rare occasions candlesticks might also be provided, but even when provided they were not customarily lighted for services. The chancel in which the altar was set might also be wainscotted, in contrast to the whitewashed nave; its floor might be paved with black and white marble; and the whole might be set off by ornamental carving in the woodwork and wrought iron. In the seventeenth century, a canopy might surmount the altar area, or the ceiling above it might receive special treatment.

While the chancel was reserved for the celebration of the sacrament, the nave was used for the liturgy of the word. Prayer Book rubrics after 1552 required the minister to lead Morning and Evening Prayer from a place where the people could hear him, and this meant erecting a reading pew for this purpose in the nave. It was generally to one side. For these purposes the clerk's pew and the pulpit were also required, and these structures might be combined in various ways—the most famous being the "three-decker" arrangement. At times they were put on two sides of the front of the nave; more frequently both were on the same side. From the reading pew the Decalogue, the Epistle, and the Gospel were also to be read at Communion or Ante-Communion, and the Litany might be led from here also. The rubrics, however, required the minister to lead the prayers of Ante-Communion or Communion from the table (they are often called "table prayers" or "altar prayers"). Puritans actively resisted this requirement, and other clergy as well were reluctant to accede to it, because it was not always easy for the congregation in the nave to see or hear the minister at the altar, particularly when it was against the east wall of the chancel. The rubric also meant that the minister had to move back and forth several times between reading desk and table—an inconvenience when the two were separated by some distance.

In the seventeenth century, the auditory church with its one-room arrangement provided a solution which enabled the congregation to see and hear the minister at the table.

Inconvenient as the requirement of reading the "table prayers" at the table was, there was an important principle behind it that high-churchmen thought worth emphasizing. In an era where a monthly celebration of the sacrament was customary, and a quarterly celebration common, the "Ante-Communion" at the altar was a "memorial" of the Holy Communion, a reminder that in the Prayer Book rite the celebration of the sacrament was intended as the climax of the worship of every Sunday and every holy day. Anthony Sparrow's *Rationale on the Book of Common Prayer,* written during the dark days of the Commonwealth when use of the Prayer Book was prohibited in England, is cited by E. C. Whitaker on this:[18]

. . .the church thereby keeping her ground, visibly minding us of what she desires and labours toward, our more frequent access to that Holy Table.

　　　　　　　　　　　　　　　　　　　CHAPTER ONE:

With all this in mind, we can see that architecture did have theological significance in the Church of England. The general care that churchmen of all schools (except the extreme Puritans) took to furnish their churches with worthy tables, suitably adorned and set off, for the celebration of the sacrament reveals an implicitly high doctrine of the eucharistic presence and the eucharistic sacrifice.

Because it was the place where Christ was made present in the sacrament, high Anglicans expected reverence for the altar. Archbishop Laud was to make this point to the members of the Order of the Garter when he preached before them, casting aside as he preached customary Anglican caution in describing Christ's presence in the sacrament:[19]

> And you, my honourable Lords of the Garter, in your great solemnities, you do your reverence, and to Almighty God, I doubt not; but yet it is *versus altare,* "towards His Altar," as the greatest place of God's residence upon earth. I say the greatest, yea, greater than the pulpit; for there it is *Hoc est corpus meum,* "This is my Body"; but in the pulpit it is at most but *Hoc est verbum meum,* "This is my Word." And a greater reverence no doubt is due to the body than to the Word of Our Lord. And so, in relation answerably to the throne where His body is usually present, than to the seat whence His Word useth to be proclaimed.

And so eucharistic doctrine comes to be worked out not only in architecture but also in ceremonial. The canons will require reverence to the altar on entering and leaving church, and some of the Laudians will astonish their opponents with their bows and genuflections before the altar. Ordinary churchpeople will seldom go so far, but they will acquire the custom of showing due reverence to the altar.

The very preference for the name altar is theologically indicative: while few Anglicans wanted to say that the priest at the altar offers Christ in a repetition of Calvary, they generally believed the Eucharist to be properly sacrificial and so the table at which it is offered is properly called an altar, and worthy of reverence for that reason as well. Lancelot Andrewes writes:[20]

> If we agree about the matter of Sacrifice, there will be no difference about the Altar. The Holy Eucharist being considered as a *Sacrifice* (in the representation of the Breaking of the Bread and pouring forth the Cup), the same is fitly called an *Altar;* which again is as fitly called a *Table,* the Eucharist being considered as a *Sacrament,* which is nothing else but a distribution and an application of the Sacrifice to the several receivers.

The high Anglican doctrine of eucharistic sacrifice may also be seen in the symbols used to adorn the altar and communion plate. From the days of Lancelot Andrewes the pelican, instruments of the passion or even the crucifix, and the Good Shepherd were popular themes—all of them with sacrificial significance. The pelican, as Horton Davies notes, is an effective symbol of the Eucharist as both sacrifice and feast, with the bird feeding her young with her own blood.[21]

The Scottish Rite

Who were the Scottish Episcopalians whose eucharistic rite was the basis for that adopted by the American church in 1789? Scottish Episcopalians had a long and complex history. The Scottish Reformation was settled on presbyterian lines in 1560, although there was provision for superintendents whose districts were generally the pre-Reformation dioceses. In 1572 provision was made for bishops, and some were ordained (by a variety of consecrators—not all of them bishops). In 1574 episcopal government was repudiated, and by 1580 these "Tulchan Bishops" had disappeared. James VI (of Scotland) and I (of the United Kingdom) imposed episcopacy on a reluctant Church of Scotland in 1610. However, the attempt of Charles I and the Scottish bishops to impose upon the Church of Scotland the 1637 liturgy led to the overthrow of the episcopacy in 1638 (and eventually to the overthrow of Charles I and the Church of England). At the Restoration, Charles II reimposed the episcopacy in 1661. When James II was overthrown in the Glorious Revolution of 1688, however, none of the Scottish bishops would take the oath of allegiance to William and Mary and the Church of Scotland once more became presbyterian in 1690. These "nonjuror" bishops eventually formed themselves into the Episcopal Church of Scotland, but because of their Jacobite sympathies they worshiped under severe restrictions until the penal laws against them were repealed in 1792.

The history of the eucharistic rite of what eventually became the Episcopal Church of Scotland is also long and complex, and we shall only sketch in the main outlines of development here. At the Reformation, the Church of Scotland adopted Knox's Book of Common Order. This was a basically Genevan rite. For our purposes it is sufficient to note that, unlike the English Prayer Books of 1552, 1559, and 1604, it carefully prescribed the manual acts, that the bread and wine are solemnly brought in and placed on the table before the reading of the institution narrative, and that while the printed rite lacks an invocation of the Spirit, this was widely felt as a lack and often supplied (since the rite did not restrict the freedom of ministers to devise their own prayer in conformity to the rubrics of the rite).

When the kingdoms of Scotland and England were united on the accession of James VI of Scotland to the throne of England as James I, a sentiment grew for greater conformity between the two churches in both their forms of church government and in their liturgies. Charles I and Archbishop Laud encouraged the Scottish bishops to prepare a Scottish edition of the English Prayer Book for this reason. The ultimate result is the Scottish Prayer Book of 1637. This has generally been called Laud's liturgy, in the belief that the Archbishop imposed his own liturgical preferences on the Scottish church. Careful scholarship now presents us with a different picture. The eucharistic liturgy in particular and the book as a whole were largely the work of the Scottish bishops, especially James Wedderburn of Dunblane, whose study had led him to a preference for the general shape of the 1549 rite. Indeed, if Wedderburn had had his way, the 1637 rite would have conformed to 1549 even more closely than it did. The more cautious Laud thought a liturgy in general conformity to the English Book of 1604 was preferable under the circumstances, although the Scottish liturgy in general was closer to his personal eucharistic theology. The cause for the rejection of this Prayer Book at this time in Scotland is probably to be sought not so much in the characteristic features of the eucharistic rite as in Puritan dislike of episcopacy, a growing Puritan dissatisfaction (in England as well as in Scotland) with fixed liturgy, and in other factors such as the Scottish distaste for saints' days, versicles and responses, and ceremonial practices such as kneeling for Communion. Puritans in both England and Scotland wanted a "root and branch" reformation that would spell the end of episcopacy and of a fixed liturgy in both countries—a kind of uniformity very different from what the king and the bishops had in mind![22]

Let us note briefly the particular features of this rite, destined to be the ultimate ancestor of the American rite. In the Proclamation of the Word of God the revisions of the English rite are minor, the chief one to note being the provision of a response to the Gospel. It was in the Celebration of the Holy Communion that

CHAPTER ONE:

the rite differed markedly from that of the English church. Its outline is as follows:

Offertory sentences (new additions)
    collection of the people's offerings
    presentation of offerings and placement on the table
    offering and placement of bread and wine on the table
Prayer for the Whole State of Christ's Church
    commemoration of departed
    commemoration of saints
Exhortation
Invitation, Confession, Absolution, Comfortable Words
Eucharistic Prayer
    Sursum Corda, Preface, Sanctus
    Prayer of Consecration
        generally that of 1549 without intercessions
        invocation conflates 1549 and 1552
        manual acts at Institution as in 1549 (no fraction)
        two titles
            Prayer of Consecration (through the Institution Narrative)
            Memorial or Prayer of Oblation (after the Institution Narrative)
Lord's Prayer
Prayer of Humble Access
Communion (1549 words of administration with "Amen")
Collect of thanksgiving
Gloria in excelsis
Blessing
Rubrics at end of service
    provision for consumption of consecrated elements
    provision for supplementary consecration

Wedderburn also desired to move the confession and related materials and the intercessions to bring the rite into even closer conformity to 1549, but did not achieve this. It will be noted that this is a rite which does conform in large part (as the English rites did not) to the classical Anglican doctrines of the eucharistic presence, consecration, and the eucharistic sacrifice: later Anglicans would wish to reshape the structure of the eucharistic prayer to resemble more closely Eastern models, but few had reached this point by 1637.

The violent rejection of the book in Scotland meant that the Book of Common Order continued in use until the English and Scottish divines of the Commonwealth hammered out the Westminster Directory for Public Worship. The eucharistic rite of the Directory is in general like that of the Book of Common Order in shape, but it is in fact a set of rubrics rather than prayers: it will go only so far as to suggest models from which the minister may compose his own prayers. In the Presbyterian tradition it specifies the manual acts; it is chiefly noteworthy for the model it proposes for the invocation of the Spirit in the consecration of the bread and wine (thus remedying a lack in Knox's book):[23]

> Earnestly to pray to God, the Father of all mercies, and God of all consolation, to vouchsafe His gracious presence, and the effectual working of His Spirit to us; and so to sanctify these elements of Bread and Wine, and to bless His own Ordinance, that we may receive by faith the Body and Blood of Jesus Christ crucified for us, and so to feed upon Him, that He may be one with us and we with him.

This, it will be noted, is a far stronger prayer than the petition for fruitful communion which replaced the invocation in English rites of 1552 and following. When the episcopacy was restored to Scotland at the Restoration, no further attempt was made to impose the Prayer Book, and the Directory remained in use. When the Scottish bishops were removed in 1690, however, the emerging Scottish Episcopal Church began to reclaim the Prayer Book tradition. Heavily influenced by their patristic scholarship and that of their nonjuring colleagues in England, the bishops began to move toward a eucharistic rite whose shape was like that of the Eastern rites they knew.

The first stage in this development was Scottish use of the 1662 English Book, which gained momentum in the reign of Queen Anne at the beginning of the eighteenth century. The Scots soon found this an inadequate rite, however, and gradually began to enrich it by moving the Prayer of Oblation from its position as an alternative postcommunion prayer to a place immediately after the Prayer of Consecration, or by using the liturgy for the Celebration of the Holy Communion from the 1637 Scottish liturgy. Quite a number of editions of this portion of the 1637 book were published from 1722 to 1764—"wee bookies," as they were known—under the title, *The Communion Office for the Church of Scotland.*

By this time, however, the Scots found the overall order of this rite, and in particular the order of the parts of the eucharistic prayer, unsatisfactory on the basis of studies of the Eastern Liturgies by them and the English Nonjurors, particularly the so-called "Clementine Liturgy" of the Apostolic Constitutions and the Liturgy of St. James. Like John Johnson, their seventeenth-century liturgical and theological precursor, they wanted a liturgy which reproduced the ancient structure. Perhaps the most learned and persuasive advocate of this position was Thomas Rattray, Bishop of Brechin and eventually Primus of the Scottish church. On the basis of his research, he drew up a liturgy for the Scottish church based on the liturgy of St. James.

It was not, however, this liturgy which Scottish Episcopalians adopted in the end. They preferred the language of Cranmer to the somewhat more exotic language of the Eastern rites. But its structure was attractive, and celebrants soon began to mark their copies of the 1637 rite so that in its celebration they rearranged its components to fit the Eastern structure. Copies of the Book marked up in this way still exist. It was only a matter of time until the 1637 structure was published in its new order. In 1735 it appeared for the first time, the change indicated (not very lucidly) by the addition on the title page of the words, "All the parts of this Office are ranked in their natural order." In addition, celebrants began to make minor adjustments in the wording of the rite to conform it to their eucharistic theology.

In 1764 this resulted in the adoption of a new eucharistic rite by the Scottish bishops.[24] This rite, like the wee bookies before it, contained only the liturgy for the Celebration of the Holy Communion. The remainder of the eucharistic rite was not published with this until 1844, although in fact the Scots came to make minor alterations to it as well (chiefly the provision of the Summary of the Law as an alternative to the Decalogue).

The following outline will reveal how completely the Cranmerian material of the 1637 rite had been rearranged to conform to the Eastern structure:

Exhortation
Offertory
  Bidding
  Sentences
  Collection of "oblations" of money and presentation
  Sentence from Chronicles as oblations are placed on table
  Offering of bread and wine and placement on Table
The Eucharistic Prayer
  Salutation, Sursum Corda, Preface, Sanctus

Prayer of Consecration
   post-Sanctus
   institution narrative with manual acts and fraction
   The Oblation (the memorial of Christ from the 1637 Prayer
      of Oblation)
   The Invocation (moved from its 1637 position)
   The remainder of the 1637 Prayer of Oblation
The Prayer for the Whole State of Christ's Church
The Lord's Prayer
Invitation, Confession, Absolution, Comfortable Words
The Prayer of Humble Access
Communion (1637 words)
Bidding and Postcommunion Prayer
Gloria in excelsis
Blessing

In addition to the new structure, the rite contained a number of small but significant changes in phrasing. When the invocation was removed from the post-Sanctus, the remainder was left dangling as a grammatical fragment. This was remedied by prefacing the words "All glory be to thee"—thus creating a verbal link between the Sanctus and the following part of the eucharistic prayer. The words which followed shortly after this, "who made there (by his one oblation of himself once offered," were changed to read "who made (by his own oblation of himself once offered)"—conforming to the nonjuring belief that Christ had offered his sacrifice at the last supper, completed it on the cross, and pleaded it in the heavenly sanctuary. In the first portion of the Prayer of Oblation from the 1637 rite the words "WHICH WE NOW OFFER UNTO THEE" were added after "gifts," thus providing an explicit oblation of the bread and wine in the eucharistic prayer. From the bidding, "Let us pray for the whole state of Christ's Church" the concluding words, "militant here in earth," were deleted, taking note of the commemoration of the departed and the saints. It should be noted that the rubric "to offer up" the bread and wine when they are placed on the table does not derive from the non-juring tradition (it is found in neither the English Nonjuror rites of 1718 and 1734 nor the rite of the Scottish Thomas Rattray) but from the 1637 Scottish rite, where it is a surviving remnant of the medieval Western rite. It also became customary to elevate the bread and wine at the upper-cased words in the Oblation of the Prayer of Consecration, however, in conformity to the Eastern rites. The result of this was a eucharistic rite that used Cranmer's language but followed the traditional Eastern structure and gave expression to characteristic high Anglican eucharistic theology. The resulting rite is probably the finest Anglican rite in use until the liturgical reforms of the latter half of the twentieth century.

It is this rite which will form the basis of the eucharistic rite of the American Book of Common Prayer in 1789.

AN APPENDED NOTE: CALVINISM AND PURITANISM

Although the question lies outside the scope of this chapter, some may wish to explore what is meant by the words "Calvinist" and "Puritan" further, since Anglicanism is not at present generally thought of as either Calvinist or Puritan.

Calvinism

John Calvin was the great theologian of the Reformation Era, and the impact of his theological writings was felt far beyond the boundaries of purely Calvinist churches. Few English Christians of the Reformation Era escaped the influence of Calvin—a fact which later ages have tended to forget.

The keystone of Calvin's doctrinal system is the doctrine of election: that those who are saved are saved because, in God's inscrutable will, God has chosen them for salvation. In its full rigor, the doctrine of absolute predestination holds that some are predestined for salvation and some are predestined for damnation ("double predestination") and that the elect who are chosen for salvation cannot fall from grace ("the perseverance of the elect"). While Article 17 sets out the general premise of predestination, holding closely to the language of Romans 8, the 39 Articles do not present the doctrine in its full Calvinist rigor. Article 2 declares that Christ is a sacrifice "not only for original guilt, but also for all actual sins of men," a belief echoed in Anglican eucharistic prayers, which affirm that Christ made on the cross "a full, perfect, and sufficient sacrifice for the sins of the whole world." This affirmation is reiterated in Article 31. These two articles echo 1 Timothy 2:4, which declares that God wills that all should be saved. Strict Calvinists would hold that Christ died only for the elect.

In the early years of the Reformation the doctrine of predestination was a matter of intense debate. While not all Anglicans held it in its full rigor, many did. Archbishop Whitgift attempted to set forth the full Calvinist doctrine in the Lambeth Articles in 1595, but Elizabeth forbade their promulgation, and they carried only the authority of their drafters. An attempt on the part of the Puritans to attach them to the 39 Articles in 1604 after the accession of James was likewise unsuccessful. Classical Anglicanism as it developed in the days of Lancelot Andrewes at the end of Elizabeth's reign and in the early Stuart era was reticent about predestination; the followers of Laud later in the Stuart era distanced themselves from the strict Calvinist doctrine in much the same way as the followers of Arminius in Holland did and so came to be known as "Arminians."

The Calvinist doctrine of election had its impact on the theology of the sacraments. Swiss Reformed theology prefers to define the sacraments as "badges or tokens of Christian men's profession" [of faith] and "certain sure witnesses . . . of grace and God's goodwill towards us," in the words of Article 25, but avoids calling them "effectual signs of grace" (in the words of the same article). There are two reasons for this. The first reason was rooted in the philosophical doctrine regarding the relation of God to creation with which Reformed theology worked: classical Catholic doctrine (followed by Lutheran theology and eventually by classical Anglican theology) holds that the created order is capable of mediating the divine presence (finitum capax infiniti); Reformed doctrine denies this (finitum non capax infiniti).

Second, the Calvinist doctrine of election means that the sacraments cannot have an instrumental efficacy, since salvation depends solely on God's election and the sacraments must therefore be only signs of grace otherwise received. In the original 42 Articles of 1553 the last paragraph of this article read: "in such only as worthily receive the same, they have a wholesome effect and operation, and yet not that of the work wrought, as some men speak. Which word, as it is strange, and unknown to Holy Scripture; so it engendereth no godly, but a very superstitious sense." The 42 Articles were in force for only a few months before the accession of Mary; when the articles were revised in 1563, this denial of instrumental efficacy was deleted, and the article now reads: "in such only as worthily receive the same, they have a wholesome effect or operation; but they that receive them unworthily, purchase to themselves damnation, as St. Paul saith."

In regard to worship, Reformed doctrine in both its Zwinglian and Calvinist forms was iconoclast in the theological sense: it rejected the use of sacred art as an aid to worship. Its position toward music in worship was similar. Zwingli rejected music altogether and removed organs from churches. Calvin does not in his *Institutes* treat the use of music in worship from a theological perspective, but in practice music in Calvinist churches was limited to unaccompanied singing of metrical psalms.

Calvinism also upheld Scripture as the sole standard for doctrine, discipline, and worship in a more rigorous manner than other churches of the Reformation. Classical Anglicanism, for which Richard Hooker was an articulate spokesman, agreed that only doctrine "which may be proved by most certain warrant of Holy Scripture" (Article 8; cf. Articles 6 and 21) may be taught as necessary to salvation. Strict Calvinism required that worship and discipline be derived directly from Scripture; Anglicanism, however, required only that "nothing be ordained contrary to God's Word" (Article 34; cf. Article 21) and so found a place for tradition. The standard of edification set out in Article 34 also implicitly gives scope for reason.

Calvin's deep eucharistic piety led him to set forth a doctrine of the eucharistic presence which stands in tension with both his doctrine of election and Reformed doctrine regarding the relation of God to creation. He advocated throughout his writings the frequent celebration of the Eucharist; his stated preference was for a weekly celebration—a preference that he was never able to put into effect in Geneva.

Calvin attempted to formulate his doctrine of the eucharistic presence in such a way as to secure its objective reality within the bounds of his own theology. For Calvin, Christ is present in the Eucharist through the power ("virtue") of the Holy Spirit: in his *Institutes* (4:17:10) Calvin writes "the Spirit truly unites things separated in space" [the bread and wine on the one hand and Christ's Body and Blood, ascended into heaven, on the other]. This presence of Christ through the power of the Spirit gives rise to the name of "virtualism" for this doctrine of the eucharistic presence. John Johnson and the Nonjurors developed this formulation of Calvin's, which finds expression in the eucharistic prayer of the Scottish rite of 1764.

When Calvin addressed the question of how the believer participates in the body and blood of Christ, he wrote (4:17:19), "I freely accept whatever can be made to express the true and substantial partaking of the body and blood of the Lord, which is shown to believers under the sacred symbols of the Supper—and so to express it that they may be understood not to receive it solely by imagination or understanding of the mind, but to enjoy the thing itself as nourishment of eternal life." This aspect of Calvin's teaching came to be known as "receptionism" for its emphasis on the presence of Christ to the faithful recipient and finds its classical spokesman in Richard Hooker.

All aspects of Calvinist doctrine have attracted support in the Church of England, although as we have seen the church's articles of belief have never unequivocally endorsed Calvinism in its full rigor. It is Calvin's doctrine of the eucharistic presence which found widest acceptance among Anglicans, although a minority of those most rigorously Calvinistic in other regards preferred the less objective doctrine of Zwingli to that of Calvin.

Puritanism

The label "Puritan" is used in a wide variety of ways by various historians of English Christianity. At the beginning of this chapter we have tried to set out what appears to be the most accurate use of the word. "Puritan" is best understood as a label for a certain theological position within the Church of England from the time of the Reformation until the restoration of the episcopacy and the Book of Common Prayer when the monarchy was restored in 1660. Before the Commonwealth, Puritans were on the whole a faction within the Church of England who worked for further reformation of its liturgy. Most wished for removal from the Prayer Book of those parts of the liturgy which they did not believe warranted by Scripture (such as the use of vestments, the sign of the cross in Baptism, the blessing of rings in matrimony, and the observance of such saints' days and feasts as were not explicitly set forth in the New Testament). They were ceremonial minimalists and preferred to restrict music in worship to unaccompanied singing of the metrical psalms. They were Calvinist in their adherence to the doctrine of election. On the whole, they wished a far stricter regime of church discipline than was established in the Church of England. They differed from one another over the matter of church polity (the proper organization and government of the church). Although Calvin himself had organized the church in Geneva along presbyterian lines, he did not rule out episcopacy as a proper form of church government. Before the Restoration, there were Puritans in the Church of England who upheld episcopal government, as well as those who preferred a presbyterian or congregationalist form of church organization. Only a minority of those who favored some form of church government other than episcopacy separated themselves from the Church of England at this time.

The Commonwealth represents the temporary triumph of the non-Episcopalians in the Church of England. With it came a more Calvinist form of worship as established by the Westminster Directory and a stricter form of Calvinist doctrine set forth in the Westminster Confession. The triumph was temporary. With the Restoration, those who were unwilling to conform to the liturgy and episcopal polity of the Church of England separated themselves from it and organized themselves either as Presbyterians or as Congregationalists. After this time the label "Puritan" is best avoided, for it has little agreed meaning. But even after this time, many Anglicans continued to hold aspects of Calvinist doctrine, particularly some form of the doctrine of election. And the Calvinist doctrine of the eucharistic presence, in either its virtualist or its receptionist form, remained the standard Anglican doctrine until the Oxford Movement.

The Church of Scotland was on the whole Calvinist in the full sense of the word. The general preference of the Scots was for a presbyterian form of church organization, although during most of the reign of the Stuarts bishops were superimposed upon the Scottish church. Until the Commonwealth, the Scots in general followed a liturgical form of celebration for the Eucharist, following John Knox's rite in the Book of Common Order. After the unsuccessful attempt by the Scottish bishops to introduce the Prayer Book of 1637, the Church of Scotland in the period of the Commonwealth and afterward followed the Westminster Directory, which is better understood as a rubrical outline for the celebration of the Eucharist than as an actual liturgy. Their eucharistic doctrine generally followed Calvin rather than Zwingli.[25]

Notes to Chapter One

BIBLIOGRAPHICAL NOTES

Texts of the liturgies described in this chapter are found in the following sources:

The First and Second Prayer Books of Edward VI, Introduction by the Right Reverend E. C. S. Gibson, New York, E.P. Dutton, 1957 (English Rites of 1549 and 1552).

Bernard Wigan, *The Liturgy in English*, London, Oxford University Press, 1962 (various rites, including the Westminster Directory and the English Rite of 1662, with textual apparatus showing variants in that rite from 1552 and 1559).

W. Jardine Grisbrooke, *Anglican Liturgies of the Seventeenth and Eighteenth Centuries*, London, SPCK, 1958 (the Scottish Rites of 1637 and 1764, the rite of Jeremy Taylor, various rites of English Nonjurors, the rite of Thomas Rattray, with commentaries).

Dom Gregory Dix in *The Shape of the Liturgy* (New York, Seabury Press, 1983) interprets the English Prayer Books of 1549, 1552, 1559, 1604, and 1662. His discussion of the eucharistic doctrine which underlay the rites raised a storm of protest, but in the end it seems essentially correct, particularly in regard to what Cranmer intended in the rite of 1552. This is the conclusion of W. Jardine Grisbrooke (in the work noted above) after reviewing the evidence, of Kenneth Stevenson (*Gregory Dix—Twenty Five Years on,* Bramcote Notts, Grove Books, 1977) and of Colin Buchanan (article on "Liturgies 4. Anglican" in J. G. Davies, editor, *The New Westminster Dictionary of Worship,* Philadelphia, Westminster Press, 1986). Paul V. Marshall, in his additional notes at the end of the Seabury edition of *The Shape,* seeks to balance Dix's picture somewhat, particularly in regard to Luther, Calvin, and Zwingli. Dix was not a sympathetic expositor of these reformers.

Useful studies of Anglican eucharistic theology in this period can be found in the commentaries in Grisbrooke's book, in Kenneth Stevenson, *Eucharist and Offering* (New York, Pueblo Publishing Company, 1986), and in Horton Davies, *Worship and Theology in England II: From Andrewes to Baxter and Fox* (Princeton, Princeton University Press, 1975). Useful excerpts from Anglican authors in this period are collected in Paul Elmer More and Frank Leslie Cross, *Anglicanism* (London, SPCK, 1957). An older though classic commentary on Anglican eucharistic theology is found in Volume II of Darwell Stone, *A History of the Doctrine of the Holy Eucharist* (New York, Longmans, Green, & Co., 1909). On the architectural setting of the rite and its theological significance, G. W. O. Addleshaw and Frederick Etchells, *The Architectural Setting of Anglican Worship* (London, Faber and Faber, 1948) is the standard work.

A useful general tool is *The New Westminster Dictionary of Liturgy and Worship,* edited by J. G. Davies (Philadelphia, Westminster Press, 1986).

NOTES ON THE TEXT

1. W. Jardine Grisbrooke, *Anglican Liturgies of the Seventeenth and Eighteenth Centuries,* pp. xii–xiii.

2. Paul Elmer More and Frank Leslie Cross, *Anglicanism,* no. 204, pp. 470–471.

3. Ibid., no. 203, p. 468.

4. Ibid., no. 199, page 463.

The Prelude to the American Rite of 1789   45

5. Louis Weil, *Sacraments & Liturgy: The Outward Signs* (Oxford, Basil Blackwell, 1983), p. 50.

6. *The Unbloody Sacrifice,* cited in Grisbrooke, p. 76.

7. *The Corruptions of the Church of Rome,* cited in Darwell Stone, *A History of the Doctrine of the Holy Eucharist,* Vol. II, page 448.

8. *The Unbloody Sacrifice,* cited in Grisbrooke, p. 81.

9. Grisbrooke, p. 71.

10. More and Cross, no. 214, p. 496.

11. *A Reply to M. Harding's Answer,* cited in Kenneth Stevenson, *Eucharist and Offering,* p. 156.

12. Grisbrooke, p. 27. It should be noted that William Forbes, first Bishop of Edinburgh after the Reformation, also bases his eucharistic doctrine on this—though his work was published posthumously and did not have the influence Taylor's was to enjoy. Cf. except no. 205 from Forbes's *Considerationes Modestae et Pacificae* in More and Cross, pp. 471–473, where he expounds the eucharistic sacrifice along these lines.

13. *The Unbloody Sacrifice,* cited in Grisbrooke, p. 74.

14. Cited in Horton Davies, p. 299.

15. *Considerationes Modestae et Pacificae,* cited above in note 12.

16. Stevenson, p. 158.

17. On architecture, see especially G. W. O. Addleshaw and Frederick Ethcells, *The Architectural Setting of Anglican Worship.* The chapters on architecture in Horton Davies, *Worship and Theology in England II,* are also useful.

18. Cited in J. G. Davies, *The New Westminster Dictionary of Liturgy and Worship,* under the article on "Ante-Communion" by E. C. Whitaker, pp. 24–25.

19. More and Cross, no. 275, p. 608.

20. More and Cross, no. 215, p. 497.

21. Horton Davies, p. 303. Cf. pp. 301–309 of this book on the matter of ceremonial and ornament.

22. The current scholarship on the history of this book is summarized in Grisbrooke, Chapter I.

23. Bernard Wigan, *The Liturgy in English,* pp. 186–187.

24. Cf. the commentary on the 1764 liturgy in Grisbrooke, Chapter VIII.

25. For Calvin's eucharistic theology, cf. *The Institutes of the Christian Religion* (volume 2 of the edition of John T. McNeill, translated by Ford Lewis Battles, Philadelphia, Westminster Press, 1940), Book 10, chapter 17; also "Short Treatise on the Lord's Supper" and "Confession of Faith Concerning the Eucharist" in *Calvin: Theological Treatises,* edited by J. K. S. Reid (Philadelphia, Westminster, nd). A. G. Dickens, *The English Reformation* (New York, Schocken Books, 1964) has a careful treatment of Puritanism in the Church of England on pages 313–321.

The Book of *Common Prayer* 1789

The Church in America at the Time of the Revolution

The Revolutionary Era of American history has generally been accounted the low ebb of religious observance in the nation's history. The loss of loyalist clergy who fled the country, and the interruption of the ministries of patriot clergy who left their parishes to support the patriot cause, dissatisfaction with the religious establishment in the colonies, the unsettled state of a society at war and also at the beginning of its westward migration, weariness with the emotional turmoil of revivalism, and the prevailing rationalistic temper of the times made serious inroads on the pattern of religious observance.

On the eve of the Revolution, the Church of England was established in Virginia and Maryland and had similar status in some other Southern colonies. Generally complacent in their legal position, Anglicans were weakened by the loss of members to denominations such as the Baptists and the Methodists, who had won large followings in the wave of revivalism in the course of the eighteenth century.

In New England, the Congregational Church was established in several colonies, and Anglicans—as a highly self-conscious minority—had developed a strong identity and a high-church outlook. Yale's entire faculty of Congregational ministers in 1722 had "studied themselves into" Anglicanism, sought ordination in England, and returned to form the beginnings of an articulate Anglican presence in a Puritan colony. Elsewhere in New England the Church of England was not so strong, and its adherents were more dependent on support from England through the Society for the Propagation of the Gospel.

In the Middle Colonies, Anglicanism was perhaps strongest in New York and New Jersey. Samuel Johnson, a "Connecticut convert," represented an articulate high churchmanship not only as a pre-Revolutionary parish priest in Connecticut but also as head of King's College (later Columbia) in New York. Elsewhere in the Middle Colonies, Anglican strength was to be found primarily in the cities (as in Philadelphia).

The impact of the Revolution was felt perhaps more severely by the former Church of England than by other denominations. Anglican clergy were bound by oath at ordination to obedience to the Crown, and the liturgy included prayers for King and Parliament. The Revolution created a crisis of conscience for these clergy and many left or suffered for their loyalty. In Virginia, independence brought disestablishment in its wake, and Chief Justice John Marshall thought the Episcopal Church in that state on the road to extinction. Everywhere, the lack of a resident American bishop left the church bereft of leadership.

After a struggle, the church organized itself in state conventions along the lines of the federal government. Eventually dioceses were able to elect and consecrate bishops, although Samuel Seabury of Connecticut had to seek ordination in Scotland because of the oath of obedience required for ordination in England; only after his consecration did parliamentary action make it possible for the Church of England to consecrate bishops for the American

50

Church. Early bishops supported themselves by continuing as parish priests—Seabury at St. James' Church, New London; White at Christ Church and St. Peter's Church, Philadelphia; New York bishops at Trinity Church, Manhattan. Bishop Madison of Virginia continued as the head of the College of William and Mary, to which he devoted most of his time and energy.

Currents of Thought

Currents of thought prevalent at the time had their own impact on Anglican and Episcopal worship. The high-church tradition, ascendant in England at the Restoration in 1660, had its strongest American presence in Connecticut and New York, where Anglicans had had to build a strong self-identity as a religious minority. Adherence to liturgical form, strong sacramental emphasis, and belief in an episcopal form of polity were distinctive of this school of thought, represented by Samuel Johnson.

Johnson's teaching is characteristic of the Anglican position in Congregational New England, a position which differed from that of the Congregational establishment in its advocacy of liturgical form and episcopal polity, but espoused a eucharistic doctrine which was essentially similar to that which had been held by the earlier Puritans of the sixteenth and early seventeenth centuries. By Johnson's time, the Congregationalists were beginning to fall away in practice from the eucharistic doctrine of their Puritan forebears which they still formally espoused. In terms of the eucharistic presence, Johnson's doctrine is perhaps best characterized as Daniel Waterland's variant of Hooker's "dynamic receptionism." In this era, such a doctrine represented for Anglicans a "middle way" between the Roman Catholic position and a Zwinglian "bare memorial." It holds to a "real presence" of Christ to the faithful communicant, but does not closely associate this presence with the sacramental bread and wine. Rationalist and revivalist forces were eroding this Calvinist position among New England Congregationalists; liturgical form served to preserve it among Anglicans. In regard to the doctrine of the eucharistic sacrifice, Johnson seems to have moved from a Calvinist to a more Anglican position, espousing a doctrine—grounded in the Christology of the epistle to the Hebrews—in which the Eucharist is a commemoration and representation of Christ's pleading the sacrifice in the heavenly sanctuary. Such teaching could be found among SPG missionaries in the Middle Colonies as well as in New England.

More important than Johnson's doctrinal similarity in his Anglican days to the eucharistic doctrine of the earlier Puritans is his difference from them in his emphasis on a sacramental and liturgical form of worship as a means of Christian nurture. He disliked both the revivalist emphasis of the neo-Calvinist Congregationalists on conversion, which found characteristic expression in forms of worship that appealed to the emotions, and the departure from orthodox faith which was characteristic of the more rationalist Congregationalists who were beginning to drift into Unitarianism. In Anglican polity and Anglican liturgy he found safeguards from both of these developments in the Congregational establishment. In the liturgical piety of Anglicanism he found a far more congenial expression of faith than in the nonliturgical piety of Congregationalism. Anglicanism's appeal in New England was to those who disliked these revivalist and unitarian trends as he did.[1]

At the other end of the spectrum, the Great Awakening in the mid-eighteenth century had created an Evangelical movement in the Church, with a stress of individual salvation and personal religion. Evangelicals were generally uncomfortable with sacramental form. John Wesley represented a strong sacramental emphasis in the evangelical movement; but others might be less sacramentally oriented, and, in any case, frontier conditions made a sacramental and liturgical emphasis hard to sustain.

The Restoration in 1660 had left many weary of the doctrinal controversies of the time, and a broader outlook became common—giving rise to the school of "latitude-men" or latitudinarians. It was an age that valued reason and was impatient with doctrinal niceties. Basil Willey writes of the Cambridge Platonists, precursors of the latitudinarians,[2] "They reject no article of the Faith, but they shift the emphasis of exhortation, affirming values where orthodoxy affirmed facts." The latitudinarians with their emphasis on reason would prove strong opponents of the Evangelicals in the eighteenth century, and often avoided the liturgical and sacramental emphasis of the high-churchmen.

John Locke, a leading philosopher of the Enlightenment, represents the rationalism of the seventeenth and eighteenth centuries in its religious form. His approach to the Bible led him to emphasize three essentials—Reason, Simplicity, and Morality.[3] The impact on worship is to be seen in the treatment of the sermon as a moral discourse and diminished emphasis on liturgical and sacramental form. Not all advocates of reason stayed within the bounds of orthodoxy. Lord Hebert of Cherbury (1583–1648) is generally considered the father of English Deism. He advocated a "religion of nature," abandoning the concept of revelation. John Tolland's *Christianity not Mysterious* (1695) and Matthew Tindal's *Christianity as Old as the Creation* (1730) were popular books that advocated deism, abandoning the incarnation and the doctrine of the Trinity. Joseph Bulter's *Analogy of Religion* (1736) and William Paley's *Evidences of Christianity* (1794) were the ablest apologies against deism, but a rationalist outlook was dominant through the period.

All of this had its impact on the American scene. Unitarian and Socinian currents were strong, and King's Chapel in Boston would become Unitarian after the Revolution, while retaining a liturgical form of worship. Many prominent Americans who were baptized Anglicans or identified themselves as Anglicans were deist in their convictions—among them Thomas Jefferson (who edited all miracles out of the New Testament) and George Washington (who refused to attend church on communion Sundays after being criticized for declining to receive the sacrament). Anglican worship on the whole was influenced enough by rationalism and latitudinarianism that it resisted revivalism in hymnody and preaching and stressed the reasonable in preaching. In New England, this attracted some Congregationalists who disliked the revivalist spirit that spread through their churches; in the South, it lost large numbers for the Episcopal Church. Episcopal worship was free from doctrinal strife and emotional excess; it could also be dull and moralistic.

The Sunday Service at the Time of the Revolution

We examined in the last chapter the textual and rubrical traditions out of which the American eucharistic rite of 1789 developed. In order to understand the eucharistic rite of 1789, however, and also to understand the goals behind the present 1979 rite, we need to consider as a part of the eucharistic rite a cluster of other rites that had been annexed to Communion (or Ante-Communion) since Archbishop Grindal's directives to the English church in 1571. Only rarely would the Eucharist have been celebrated without these rites as a constituent part of the service on Sundays or feast days. Sunday morning worship before and after the adoption of the First American Prayer Book in 1789 would have consisted of Morning Prayer (with Baptism if there were children to be baptized), the Litany, Ante-Communion with sermon, and (for those who "tarried" on the Sundays when it was administered) Communion. Morning Prayer, the Litany, and Ante-Communion

54

were all part of what the Book of Common Prayer 1979 calls "The Proclamation of the Word of God."

This seems a large dose of worship for Sunday mornings, and it was, but Christians of all denominations were accustomed to devoting far more of their Sundays to worship than we are today. Nevertheless, Morning Prayer and Ante-Communion were not designed to be joined as a single service. When the full Sunday morning service was celebrated prior to the adoption of the 1789 Book, there would be an enormous amount of duplication in the components of the combined rite:

6 repetitions of the Lord's Prayer (4 on Sundays without baptism or communion)

2 recitations of the Apostles' Creed (one on Sundays without baptism)

the Nicene Creed as well as the Apostles' Creed

2 confessions (one on Sundays without communion)

4 lessons (1 Old Testament, 3 New Testament)

1 additional lesson on Sundays with baptism

2 intercessions

the Litany
the Prayer for the Church (perhaps sometimes omitted when there was no Communion)

As we can see, the problem was as much duplication of material as it was the length of the service. No wonder the Puritans accused Anglicans of vain repetitions in their liturgy! Moreover, the components did not fit together smoothly as a continuous service. The Litany functions as an appropriate intercession with Morning Prayer, but the opening of Ante-Communion represents thematically a "second beginning" to worship.

From 1789 to 1979 the Episcopal Church would strive to create a comprehensive service of Word and Sacrament for Sundays and feast days. Not until 1979, however, would all the original components be integrated into a single unified service. Up until that time, the Church addressed the problem by allowing abbreviation of the components or even (after 1856) separation of the components for celebration as distinct services. Before 1979, however, Sunday worship was greatly impoverished when the components were separated, as we shall see in later chapters.

The matter of how frequently the sacrament was administered merits somewhat fuller discussion. The rite of 1552, which in other respects is a low-water mark in Anglican eucharistic doctrine, nevertheless presupposes a weekly celebration with communicants. In cathedral and collegiate churches, which had many ministers on their staffs, it requires those ministers to communicate each Sunday. Even in parish churches, the rubric which stipulates that the service be terminated after the Prayer for the Whole State of Christ's Church when the number of communicants is insufficient makes provision for this contingency only on "the holy days," not on Sundays. However, the Church of England had no more success in achieving a weekly celebration than did such other reformers as Calvin; in an era where people had been accustomed to communicate once a year, it was not easy to effect so great a change in people's piety and practice. As a result, the sacrament generally came to be celebrated monthly in town churches, and usually quarterly in country churches. At Easter season, when all were required to communicate, and at other times when they were accustomed to do so, it was often necessary to provide several celebrations to make this possible. At times this might be an evening celebration—a custom that died out in the nineteenth century under the impact of Tractarian emphasis on fasting Communion. Good Friday was a common additional celebration for the Easter Communion.

Both high-churchmen and evangelicals desired a celebration more frequently than quarterly. Both in England and in this country there were occasional attempts to provide a weekly celebration by scheduling it on a different Sunday of the month in each of the different parishes of a town, or by establishing a rotation among several churches within a single cure. Such provisions were exceptional, however. Evangelicals and Puritans have an undeservedly bad reputation on this matter. The English independents who were the precursors of the New England Congregationalists seem to have aimed at a weekly celebration of the sacrament, while John Cotton reports that in New England it is administered once a month. John and Charles Wesley, leaders of the Evangelical Revival, were fervent sacramentalists. John customarily received communion at least twice a week over the course of his ministry, and one of Charles Wesley's hymns for the Lord's Supper laments the cessation of the "daily sacrifice" as a sign of decay. On the whole, the Evangelicals can be credited with moving the church toward a monthly celebration as a minimum standard. Less frequent celebration is to be attributed to latitudinarian laxity more than any other cause, though by no means all of the latitudinarians neglected the sacraments.

For music, American Anglicans before and after 1789 relied almost exclusively on the metrical psalter (all 150 psalms versified) for hymnody. The version most frequently used by the middle of the eighteenth century was the "New Version" of Tate and Brady, which replaced the "Old Version" of Sternhold and Hopkins. The texts of the metrical psalms were frequently bound up with both English and American Prayer Books. These "singing psalms" left much to be desired as poetry—the reason that almost none have survived in our present hymnal. Americans began to supplement metrical psalms with other hymns much earlier than English Anglicans. The Proposed Book of 1786 had a collection of 51 hymns and a reduced repertoire of only 84 metrical psalms. The more conservative preference of William White prevailed in the 1789 Prayer Book, however, and the full metrical psalter was bound up with the Prayer Book, while the selection of hymns was reduced to 27. The appeal of metrical psalms was on the decline, however; by 1808 the number of hymns in the Prayer Book collection had risen to 58. By 1826, 212 hymns were included. Many of the early hymns were drawn from Baptist and Independent sources, such as Watts and Doddridge. In the early nineteenth century, sources included English Evangelicals and American churchmen.

A few tunes might be included in a separate section of the psalters (the Proposed Book of 1786 included eight pages of tunes), but tunes were more frequently published separately in "tune books," which the parish clerk would use for "lining out" the psalms—singing them line by line, with the congregation repeating each line after him. Gradually, during the eighteenth and early nineteenth centuries, this method was supplanted by unison or harmonized singing by the congregation as a whole (usually supported by a parish choir in the gallery and an organ or other instruments). Organs in churches at first distinguished Anglicans from the Puritans, who long resisted instrumental music. Singing schools were sometimes organized to train congregations to sing the hymnody. At this time, the melody of the hymn was customarily written in the tenor part, not in the soprano as today. Until a resolution by the House of Bishops directed the congregation to stand for hymns in 1814, it had generally been customary to sing them seated—a custom that made some sense when the metrical psalms were "lined out." In rare cases, orphanages or schools might provide the resources for a boys' choir or a children's choir in a parish. More common in larger parishes as the nineteenth century progressed was the quartet choir—a quartet consisting of a soloist for each part. Hymns or metrical psalms might be sung, according to royal injunctions and a similar rubric in the first American Book of Common Prayer, before and after services (that is, the component rites of the Morning Service) and sermons.

Some service music might also be sung in parishes with adequate musical resources—the canticles at Morning Prayer (and less frequently the prose psalms), and perhaps the Sanctus (often called at this period the Trisagion) and the Gloria in excelsis at Communion. The 1789 rubric permitting the substitution of a hymn for the Gloria is probably an indication, however, that this text was beyond the abilities of many parishes. A fuller sung service was customary in English cathedrals and collegiate churches, but such institutions did not exist in the colonies. Even in England, the "ordinary" of the Eucharist, apart from the Gloria in excelsis and at times the Decalogue and the Nicene Creed, was seldom sung. The Sanctus, when sung with the 1662 rite, had come to be used between the Litany and the Communion. Such service music as there was was likely to be largely manuscript or printed in tune books. The early nineteenth century saw a proliferation of books of service music. Official regulation or publication of hymn tunes and service music was still far in the future, however.

The visual foci of the rite were customarily the reading pews and pulpit, on the one hand, and the holy table on the other. The service would be led by the minister and the parish clerk from their "reading pews" and the pulpit (generally all of these were combined in a single structure—the "three-decker"). It was probably not customary in most places for the minister to go to the holy table for the Ante-Communion—especially when the sacrament was not to follow.[4] When the sacrament was administered, at the offertory the minister would go and stand at the north end of the table. To us, the rite would appear quite "static," with far less movement than we are accustomed to. Minister and clerk would enter and depart informally without procession. Apart from this, the minister would move only to enter the pulpit for the sermon and to go to the holy table for the sacrament. In many, perhaps most, places the custom of "drawing near" at the offertory would have fallen into disuse by the time of the Revolution, and the people would approach the table only at the time of Communion.

Ceremonially, the minister would use only such actions as were indicated by the rubrics of the book and were functionally necessary for the conduct of the service. For services, he would wear surplice (to which tippet and hood might be added); for the sermon, he would change to a gown. In places, some ministers (particularly Puritan Anglicans and Scottish Episcopalians) conducted all services in gowns; in others, they may not have changed to gown for the sermon. Surplices in this period were ankle-length garments; the cassock customarily worn under them was frequently omitted.

The discussion of architecture which follows will be facilitated if the reader will refer to the schematic architectural plans in the appendix. In early Southern churches, the "two-room" style of the "Gothic survival" in church architecture can be found. The term "Gothic survival" indicates the persistence of elements of Gothic design after other styles came to predominate; "Gothic revival" is used to indicate the later conscious imitation of the Gothic style. Elsewhere, and later in the South, buildings were generally of the "one-room" variety. Choirs were invariably in a gallery or in nave pews, not in the chancel. They were (with rare exceptions) not vested.

Reading pew and holy table might be arranged in a variety of ways in the churches: the holy table was almost always at the center of the chancel at the front, but the reading pew and/or pulpit might be on the side wall of the church (especially in "Gothic survival" plans), behind the table, or even in front of or above it. In St. Peter's Church in Philadelphia, the reading pew/pulpit is at the center of one end of the church, the table at the center of the opposite end. Anglicans would generally take pains to see that the table was covered with a decent "carpet" at all times and with a fair linen for the sacrament. It would have neither cross nor candles for ornament, however, and flowers would not be in use. There might be a hanging for the pulpit. For table and pulpit hangings, no sequence of liturgical colors was used. Baptismal fonts were likely to be placed at the front of the church. Box pews were generally in use, and pew rents were customary.

The Eucharist in the Book of Common Prayer 1789

The last chapter reviewed the primary sources of the text and rubrics of the American eucharistic rite of 1789. English material from the Prayer Book of 1662 formed the basis of the book and entered it through the somewhat latitudinarian revision known as the Proposed Book of 1786. In this form it was used for several years on a trial basis in much of the American church. The Scottish Communion Office of 1764 came before General Convention largely by way of Bishop Seabury's Communion Office, but support for this office came from elsewhere also. The Maryland and Pennsylvania conventions had supported the restoration of an invocation to the eucharistic prayer (in the English position, before the institution narrative). William Smith, a Scottish priest who served in Maryland, Rhode Island, and—later—Connecticut, wrote in support of the use of the Scottish prayer. Another William Smith (of Maryland and Pennsylvania) read the prayer with effective eloquence to the house of deputies at Convention, where he served as president. Samuel Parker of Boston also supported the Scottish prayer.

We will look first at an outline of the Sunday Service in the Book of Common Prayer 1789, and then turn to look at sources of the variants from the 1662 rite. We look at the entire Sunday Service rather than simply the eucharistic rite, because (as we have seen) Morning Prayer, Litany, and Ante-Communion or Holy Communion formed one continuous Sunday rite in Anglican usage, and because we need to look at all its components to understand some of the principles behind the revision of the eucharistic rite by the American church in 1979.

The Proclamation of the Word of God

Morning Prayer
    Sentences
    Invitation, Confession, Absolution
    The Lord's Prayer
    Preces or Opening Versicles (omitting the second English
        set)
    Venite (ending with cento from Psalm 96)
    Psalms of the Day or Psalm Selection
    Gloria Patri or Gloria in excelsis at end of psalms
    First Lesson
    Te Deum or Benedicite
    Second Lesson
    (Baptism—shortened except one Sunday a month)
    Jubilate or 4 verses of Benedictus Dominus Deus
    Apostles' or Nicene Creed
    Salutation, first and last sets of English suffrages or versicles
    Collect for day (except when Communion office follows)
    Fixed Collects, Prayer for President
    The Litany (portion from Agnus Dei to last prayer may be
        omitted)
Ante-Communion

CHAPTER TWO:

Lord's Prayer with doxology (optional when Morning
    Prayer precedes)
Collect for Purity
Decalogue with Responses
Summary of the Law (optional addition to Decalogue)
Decalogue Collect (optional)
Collect of the Day
Epistle
Gospel (with initial response)
Rubric requiring Apostles' or Nicene Creed if Morning
    Prayer has not preceded
Announcements and Sermon

The Celebration of the Holy Communion

Offertory Sentences and Collection of Alms
Presentation of Alms
Preparation and Placement of the Bread and Wine on the
    Altar
Prayer for the Whole State of Christ's Church ("here in
    earth" omitted)
Exhortation
Invitation, Confession, Absolution, Comfortable Words
Sursum Corda, First Part of Preface (Proper Preface when
    appointed)
Second Part of Preface and Sanctus (both said by the peo-
    ple)
Prayer of Humble Access
Prayer of Consecration with Oblation and Invocation
Hymn and Communion
Lord's Prayer, postcommunion prayer
Gloria in excelsis or hymn
Blessing

We will consider features new to this rite (in comparison to 1662) under several headings:

1. Proposals to abridge the Sunday morning service;

2. Proposals to simplify doctrine;

3. Proposals for enrichment;

4. Proposals to remove archaisms.

1. Proposals to Abridge the Sunday Morning Service: When political change made it necessary for the American church to revise the Book of Common Prayer, there was a widespread desire to eliminate some of the duplications and repetitions in the Sunday morning service. Suggestions about how to achieve this had been put forth in England for more than a century; such suggestions are usually accounted latitudinarian, but in fact they were advocated by churchmen of all schools. Several provisions for abridging the service were incorporated in the 1786 Proposed Book; many of these became part of the Book of Common Prayer in 1789, while others were modified or rejected. The 1789 Book itself incorporated other provisions for abridgement not found in the 1786 Book.

In Morning Prayer, the second set of versicles in the preces or opening versicles was omitted. The Gloria Patri was required only in the preces and at the conclusion of the psalmody; it was optional with individual psalms and canticles. The Benedictus (untouched in 1786) was reduced to four verses. The threefold Kyrie and the Lord's Prayer were deleted and the suffrages (intercessory versicles after the creed) were reduced to the first and last sets of versicles from the English rite. The collect of the day was to be omitted when the Communion office was to follow.

The baptismal office was shortened by removing the interrogative form of the creed. One of the initial prayers and the use of the sign of the cross were made optional. The Gospel in the office, and the address and prayer following it, as well as the short petitions after the promises, might also be omitted, provided that they were used one Sunday a month.

In the revised Litany, all the material from the Agnus Dei to the last prayer might be omitted.

In Ante-Communion, the initial Lord's Prayer (to which the doxology was restored) might be omitted when Morning Prayer had preceded (according to the rubrics of the book, this would occur only in celebrations for the sick). This had been altogether omitted in 1786. In 1786 the Nicene Creed had been omitted; in 1789 it was printed in Morning Prayer and a rubric was inserted requiring that the Apostles' or Nicene Creed be said at Communion if not used at Morning Prayer. On Sundays when the sacrament was not celebrated, Ante-Communion ended with the Gospel (and presumably the sermon, though the rubric does not say so), instead of with the Prayer for the Whole State of Christ's Church (as in the English rite).

2. **Proposals to Simplify Doctrine:** The rationalistic temper of the times and the Puritan preference for formulation of Christian doctrine in biblical terms created a desire on the part of many to eliminate more complex metaphysical statements of the faith and also condemnatory expressions in the Prayer Book. The exhortation at the Eucharist was revised for these reasons, and the 1786 Book eliminated the Nicene Creed (restored in 1789) and the Athanasian Creed (not restored). In 1789 (not 1786, however) this desire led likewise to making use of a proper preface on Trinity Sunday optional and providing as an alternative to the traditional preface for that day one couched in more biblical terms. The word "minister" was often used in preference to "priest" to avoid giving offense. Changes in the wording of the catechism also affected the church's eucharistic teaching, somewhat weakening the doctrine of the eucharistic presence.

3. Proposals for Enrichment: In the Venite at Morning Prayer, a cento of verses from Psalm 96 replaces the last section of Psalm 95. For the use of the Psalms in monthly course, the minister may substitute a group of psalms from a table of Psalm Selections. In 1786 psalm selections had replaced the full psalter altogether. The church in years to come would continue to seek a solution to the problem of appropriate office psalmody; eventually the provision of psalms in the office lectionary was found the best way of addressing the issue.

In 1789 provision was made for use of the Gloria in excelsis in place of the Gloria Patri to conclude the psalmody. Several factors may have entered into this provision. It avoided repetition of the Gloria Patri, already used in the preces. It allowed regular use of the Gloria in excelsis, which would not often have been used at a time when the sacrament was celebrated infrequently. It may also have been a way of getting the Gloria in excelsis into the chant repertoire through more frequent use.

The principal enrichment in the eucharistic rite was the adoption of a full eucharistic prayer with oblation and invocation, based on that of the Scottish rite of 1764. This was slightly revised for theological reasons. The phrase "one oblation" was restored from the English rite in preference to the Scottish "own oblation" in the post-Sanctus. In addition, the invocation took the form proposed by the Maryland and Pennsylvania conventions with a petition for fruitful reception, not consecration (though it was put in the Scottish, not the English position).

The Prayer of Humble Access was left in the English position after the Sanctus, and the English rather than the Scottish order for other components of the service was followed. The adoption of the Scottish eucharistic prayer should be credited, as we have seen, to the efforts of others as well as those of Samuel Seabury. Surprisingly, it was presented as a safeguard against the doctrine

CHAPTER TWO:

of transubstantiation—perhaps because the English prayer, lacking an invocation, of necessity treats the words of institution as consecratory.

Other enrichments in the American rite include the optional addition of the Summary of the Law to the Decalogue (perhaps the original intention was to make it an alternative), which was taken from Scottish usage along with the use of the Decalogue collect to replace the collect for the King. The response to the Gospel also follows Scottish usage (it may have continued in the English rite by unwritten custom as well). A rubric was added allowing the people to join in the last portion of the Preface and the Sanctus (another formalization of unwritten custom). The use of a hymn after the eucharistic prayer was a final enrichment.

4. Removal of Archaisms: Numerous improvements were made in the wording of the Book of Common Prayer in 1789. "Who" consistently replaces "which" as a relative personal pronoun. "Be" as an indicative form was replaced by "are." We are familiar with this updating in the Lord's Prayer and the Collect for Purity. Similar revisions were made in the Te Deum, the psalms, and elsewhere.

Changes in the prayers for civil authority which necessitated the revision were made throughout the book.

In a similar way, rubrics were conformed to prevailing usage. Permission was given to lead Ante-communion from the reading desk—a common custom from the seventeenth century on. Permission to sing a hymn in place of the Gloria in excelsis at Communion probably arose from the fact that many parishes lacked musical resources or training to sing the canticle.

Musical provisions remained much the same as before, although the metrical psalms were now frequently supplemented by other hymns. A partial metrical psalter and 51 other hymns were bound up with the Proposed Book; in 1789 a full metrical psalter and 27 other hymns were included. The Proposed Book had included hymn tunes and chant tunes; however, it was generally only the texts for the "singing psalms" that were bound up with the Prayer Book. Many parishes continued to supplement hymnody from other sources. The transition from the lining out of hymns by the parish clerk to the present style of congregational hymnody (supported by organ or other instruments and choir), which had begun earlier in the century, was well under way. Various tune books provided music for both hymns and the service music (restricted in this period, when it was used, to the canticles for the most part).

The 1789 Rite in Use: Developments

Parish worship on the whole continued along prerevolutionary lines once the Episcopal Church had organized itself and adopted a Prayer Book. Regional variations persisted. Connecticut's Bishop Seabury devoted himself energetically to his episcopal ministry, ordaining clergy for New England, making episcopal tours to administer confirmation (a rite previously unknown in a colonial church without bishops), and urging more frequent celebration and reception of Communion. When Seabury was consecrated in Scotland, his eucharistic theology seems to have been of the ordinary high-church kind characteristic in Connecticut in his day. But the Scots sent him back with a collection of pamphlets and books which set forth their own distinctive outlook, and in the next few years he seems to have adopted this outlook in its entirety. Others share with him the credit for the adoption of a variant of the Scottish eucharistic prayer in the 1789 Prayer Book, but none seem to have so consistently advocated the theology to which that text gives expression as Seabury did. He issued in 1789 *An Earnest Persuasive to Frequent Communion* and in 1791 reprinted the catechism of the Scottish bishop George Innes of Brechin, which lists as first of the duties of the sabbath "to offer and receive the Holy Eucharist." In New London, he himself adopted the practice of a celebration each Sunday. He was ahead of his time, however, and was unsuccessful in persuading others to follow his example.

Similar evidence for the theological outlook of "Connecticut Churchmen" can be found in the office for the induction of ministers first used for the induction of William Smith (who had now moved from Rhode Island) in Norwalk. A form of this service was added to the Prayer Book in 1804. The theological vocabulary of this service is markedly different from that of the rest of the Prayer Book: here we find such terms as "sacerdotal function," "presbyter," "altar," and "Holy Eucharist" which are characteristic of the Scottish nonjuring tradition but were generally avoided in the Prayer Book. It is the eucharistic tradition of this Connecticut churchmanship which made the teaching of the early tracts (which we will review in the next chapter) unremarkable to American high-churchmen.

In New York, John Henry Hobart became first the assistant and then the successor to Benjamin Moore as Bishop of New York. Able and energetic, he traveled throughout the state organizing churches, administering confirmation, creating societies to provide Prayer Books and religious literature, distributing tracts to set forth the case of the Episcopal Church, and setting up the General Seminary and Geneva (later Hobart) College. His churchmanship had a more English cast to it than Seabury's, and, much as Samuel Johnson had, he stressed "evangelical truth and apostolic order." He upheld strict adherence to liturgical form and advocated a style of architecture that placed altar, pulpit, and reading desk in prominent positions in the front of the church, arranged with pulpit and desk *behind* the altar so that they did not block the view of the altar from the nave, as a three-decker in the central aisle in front of the altar frequently did. He favored an early "Gothic revival" style of architecture—distinct from the later Gothic revival by the absence of a separate "room" for a chancel. He taught churchmen to value confirmation and communion highly, but in his maturity his eucharistic teaching on the whole did not follow the nonjuring and Scottish tradition of Bishop Seabury. Early in his ministry, he espoused nonjuring views like those of Seabury, having learned them from reading John Johnson and George Hickes; but later he followed William White in rejecting them for the teaching of Waterland, which was prevalent in the American church of his day. His stress on "apostolic order" and his apologetic use of patristic literature provides a link to the later teaching of the Oxford tracts, while his eucharistic doctrine distinguishes him from them. He might be said to have combined Samuel Johnson's theology with Samuel Seabury's energy.[5] *The Churchman,* a journal which he endorsed and which later had Bishop Seabury's grandson, Samuel Seabury, Jr., as its editor, became the unofficial voice of the high-churchmen. In this era Bishop Dehon of South Carolina represented a similar strand of high-churchmanship in the Southern states.

In Alexander Viets Griswold of Massachusetts (the Eastern Diocese), Philander Chase of Ohio (and later Illinois), and Richard Moore of Virginia, the Evangelicals found strong episcopal leadership. These men put less stress on the church's liturgy and tradition and more on evangelical outreach in a freer, less liturgical style more like that of other Protestant denominations. They were apt to supplement the Prayer Book services with less formal preaching services and to practice open Communion.

Latitudinarians really did not constitute a distinct liturgical tradition at this period in the church's history. Some, like Bishop White, were in their own way high-churchmen, were conscientious in their sacramental life, and resisted the newer evangelical hymnody, while moving toward a greater use of chant in the liturgy. Others sat loose to the rubrics and in their rationalistic outlook minimized the importance of the sacraments. Still others showed the influence of their more evangelical colleagues. On the whole, however, divisions within the church were more doctrinal than liturgical in the early nineteenth century. Churchmen of all schools professed loyalty to the Prayer Book and worshipped in a similar, relatively unceremonious fashion. What distinguished high-churchmen from evangelicals in this period was primarily where they placed their emphasis: high-churchmen emphasized what distinguished the Episcopal Church from other denominations—"apostolic order" and a fixed liturgy—and in general kept aloof from other churches; evangelicals, while accepting apostolic order and the liturgical tradition, placed the emphasis on what the Episcopal Church shared with other churches of the Reformation and worked more closely with them. With the publication of the *Tracts for the Times*, starting in 1833, and the Gothic Revival as espoused by the Cambridge Camden Society, all this was to change.

But that is part of the story of the Prayer Book of 1892 in the next chapter.

Notes to Chapter Two

BIBLIOGRAPHIC NOTES

The text of the 1789 eucharistic rite is most easily accessible by following the critical apparatus to the 1928 rite in Bernard Wigan, *The Liturgy in English*

(London, Oxford University Press, 1962). For Morning Prayer, the Litany, and Baptism, the general outlines of the texts can be followed in Marion J. Hatchett, *The Making of the First American Book of Common Prayer* (New York, Seabury, 1982).

Hatchett's book is the standard work on this rite. It corrects in some instances errors in the generally good treatment of the rite in *Prayer Book Studies IV* (New York, Church Pension Fund, 1957). Two articles in Malcolm C. Bursin, editor, *Worship Points the Way* (New York, Seabury, 1981)—Samuel M. Garrett, "Prayer Book Presence in Colonial America," and H. Boone Porter, "Toward an Unofficial History of Episcopal Worship"—also treat this period.

Sydney Ahlstrom, *A Religious History of the American People* (2 volumes, Garden City, Image/Doubleday, 1975) sets the period in the perspective in American history. Trends of thought in the period in England may be studied in the brief treatment in John R. H. Moorman, *A History of the Church in England* (London, Adam and Charles Black, 1963). Basil Willey has fine essays on the Cambridge Platonists, John Locke, and others in *The Seventeenth Century Background* (Garden City, Doubleday Anchor, n.d.).

The eucharistic theology of Samuel Johnson is studied in Louis Weil's unpublished 1972 doctoral thesis for the Institut Catholique, Paris, "Worship and Sacraments in the Theology of Samuel Johnson." The eucharistic theology of Daniel Waterland, on which Johnson depended, can be studied in Darwell Stone, *The Theology of the Holy Eucharist,* volume II (London, Longmans, Green, and Co., 1909). Bruce E. Steiner, *Samuel Seabury: A Study in the High Church Tradition* (Athens, Ohio, Ohio University Press, 1974) is the standard work on Connecticut's first bishop; Anne Rowthorn also treats his teaching on the eucharist in her shorter work, *Samuel Seabury: A Bicentennial Biography* (New York, Seabury, 1983). For John Henry Hobart's teaching, see Robert Bruce Mullin, *Episcopal Vision/American Reality: High Church Theology and Social Thought in Evangelical America* (New Haven, Yale, 1986).

There is no systematic study of the architecture of Episcopal churches in this country known to the author, although there are several regional surveys. Because parishes adapt the architectural setting for their worship to the prevailing fashion of the day, few buildings retain their original design in all details. Studies of Virginia churches give evidence of original "two-room" designs for early churches. Trinity Church, Newport, Rhode Island, retains the predominant arrangement of the period with its "three-decker" structure for reading desks and pulpit. Other churches are listed in the text of this chapter, though most have undergone some subsequent change. The Hobartian chancel is briefly described with a print and ground plan in *The Christian Journal,* volume 11, number 5, pages 134–135 (May 1827). Similar arrangements can still be seen in some New England and New York churches.

The most useful of the regional surveys are those of Vernon Perdue Davis and James Scott Rawlings (*Virginia's Colonial Churches* (1963), *Virginia's Ante-Bellum Churches* (1978), and *The Colonial Churches of Virginia, Maryland, and North Carolina: Their Interiors and Worship* (1985), published by the Dietz Press in Richmond. The last volume treats not only the architecture but the worship, and gives a carefully researched sense of what worship was like in the prerevolutionary period, treating ceremonial and music as well as purely architectural questions. It is, in fact, the best treatment that the author knows of the character of worship during this period. Equally valuable is Dell Upton, *Holy Things and Profane* (MIT Press, Cambridge, MA, 1986), in which Virginia's churches are subjected to professional architectural investigation.

The history of hymnody in this period receives brief but careful treatment in Mason Martens's essay, "Four Centuries of Anglican Hymnody in America," in *Hymnal Studies One* (New York, Church Hymnal Corporation, 1982). The history of music in the Episcopal Church is also covered in Leonard Ellinwood, *The History of American Church Music* (New York, Morehouse-Gorham Co., 1953) and *The Hymnal 1940 Companion* (New York, Church Pension Fund, 1949 and subsequent editions). The reader should be warned that the history of service music is only now being studied in a systematic way; it will receive more adequate treatment in the Companion to the Hymnal 1982, whereas it was largely overlooked in the Companion to the 1940 Hymnal. Such study depends heavily on research into tune books, manuscripts, and programs preserved in parish libraries, and similar collections. The author acknowledges assistance on this matter from Raymond Glover of Church Hymnal Corporation; Elizabeth Morris Downie, Chair of the Standing Commission on Church Music; and Marion Hatchett.

NOTES ON THE TEXT

1. Cf. Louis Weil's doctoral thesis on Samuel Johnson listed in the bibliographic note. The author acknowledges his thanks to Dr. Weil for making this manuscript available to him. Dr. Donald Gerardi examines the difference of the sacramental piety of Johnson from that of New England Congregationalists in "Samuel Johnson and the Yale 'Apostasy' of 1722: The Challenge of Anglican

Sacramentalism to the New England Way," in *The Historical Magazine of the Protestant Episcopal Church,* vol. XLVII, no.2, June 1978.

2. Basil Willey, *The Seventeenth Century Background,* page 143.

3. John R. H. Moorman, *A History of the Church in England,* pages 256–257.

4. Cf. Landon Carter's remark about his rector, ". . . he goes to the Alta[r] as seldom in the church service [to pray] as any Min[is]ter I have ever been acquaint[ed] with," quoted in Dell Upton, *Holy Things and Profane,* page 96. This clergyman also apparently preferred baptisms in church after the service to those during the service, which would require him to leave the reading desk and then return to it.

5. Cf. the treatment of Hobart in Robert Bruce Mullin, *Episcopal Vision/American Reality.* In remarking on the "English cast" of his churchmanship, the author means to distinguish it from the nonjuring theology of Seabury. Hobart studied the theology under the tutelage of William White, whose course of study was highly eclectic. The author wishes to acknowledge his gratitude to the Rev. Charles Henery of Nashotah House for assistance with material on Bishop Hobart.

CHAPTER TWO:

The Book *of Common Prayer* 1892

Tractarians, the Romantic Movement, and the Architectural Revolution

From 1607 until the 1830s Anglican and Episcopal Sunday worship and the shape of the Sunday Eucharist maintained a remarkable degree of consistency and uniformity. Musical styles shifted from the Old to the New Version of the metrical psalter and then to a greater use of other hymnody; more service music came into use, parish choirs replaced the clerk who lined out the hymns, and use of organs and other instruments became more common. With the Book of Common Prayer 1789 the texts of the liturgy underwent modest revision, although the theological significance of the American eucharistic prayer was probably not evident to most communicants. Architectural styles shifted somewhat also, but after a few buildings in the very early period in the "two-room" Gothic survival style, "one-room" styles with similar arrangements of reading desk, pulpit, and holy table prevailed. Celebrations of the Eucharist became somewhat more frequent under the influence of early Evangelicals, although the sacramental minimalism of rationalism was a countervailing force. Still, the eucharistic rite in the 1830s was celebrated in a similar style by all schools of churchmanship—a style in recognizable continuity to what had been customary since the days of the settlement in Jamestown.

The *Tracts for the Times* shattered this liturgical uniformity, and Anglican worship was, from the time of their publication, fragmented for more than a century and a half. From this time on, various schools of churchmanship (and different groups within those schools) would diverge from one another radically in eucharistic piety, theology, and ceremonial. By the end of the nineteenth century, the style of eucharistic celebration that had been standard at the beginning of the century had been abandoned by all schools.

The *Tracts for the Times* were a series that began in 1833, issued by English clergy at Oxford who were rediscovering the Catholic tradition in Anglicanism. These "Oxford Reformers" and their disciples came to be known by a wide variety of names: Tractarians (from the *Tracts for the Times*), Ritualists (from their later ceremonial—or ritual—usages), Puseyites (from Edward Pusey, their leader after the defection of John Henry Newman to the Roman Catholic Church), and Anglo-Catholics. In the United States, a collection of the early tracts was published with the endorsement of Bishop Benjamin Onderdonk of New York, a high-churchman in the tradition of John Henry Hobart. At first the tracts caused little serious stir in the American Church. The faculty of General Seminary, who made use of them in their classes, found little in them that departed from their own high-church roots in Anglican tradition.

The heart of early Tractarian theology was a consistent development of the earlier high-church tradition. It insisted on a high view of the church as the instrument of divine grace and of the ministry as an apostolic ordinance, on a high view of the sacraments as important means of grace, and on a high view of Christ's presence in the eucharist and of the sacrificial nature of the eucharist. John and Charles Wesley had held a very high sacramental doctrine, rooted in the older high-church tradition, and from one point of view the Tractarians stand in succession to them. Yet the later Evangelical movement was to emphasize inner religion in a way that minimized the importance of liturgical form and sacramental expression, and Tractarians and Evangelicals were destined to diverge dramatically from each other in their sacramental theology. The strength of both Evangelicals and Tractarians, however, was their appeal to the heart as well as the mind of believers, and their advocacy of a life of disciplined holiness. Both found their success in ministering to a church that had been emotionally starved by the excesses of a desiccated rationalism.

Tract 90, which appeared in 1841, was different, and it signals at once to us what is to distinguish Tractarian or Anglo-Catholic high-churchmanship from the older American high-churchmanship in the tradition of Andrewes, Laud, and Cosin and the Nonjurors and Scottish Episcopalians. In Tract 90, Newman seeks to show that the teaching of the 39 Articles need not necessarily be at variance with the medieval Catholic doctrine properly understood. Startling as this project seems, it was neither completely unprecedented nor totally unwarranted. In the seventeenth century, Christopher Davenport, an Englishman who had become a Franciscan had argued the same position from the Roman Catholic side. The 39 Articles had been drafted to set the doctrinal limits of the Church of England. They represent, among other things, a repudiation of medieval distortions of Catholic doctrine. The decrees of the Council of Trent, issued at the end of the sixteenth century, were a Roman Catholic attempt to deal with many of the same distortions and abuses and with the Reformation response to them.

Tract 90 signals the beginning of a shift from the tractarian espousal of the Anglican Via Media as a "middle way" between Rome and Geneva, between Roman Catholicism and classical

Protestantism, to later tractarian readiness to take Tridentine Roman Catholicism, with minor variations, as the doctrinal standard. No longer would the Tractarians think of themselves as "Protestant and Reformed according to the ancient Catholic Church" in the words of John Cosin. Because the Tractarians wanted to stress the continuity of the post-Reformation Church of England with the pre-Reformation Church, their view of the Reformation was basically negative, and they sought to minimize its importance and normative character in Anglican doctrine and Anglican liturgy. While they would continue to appeal to the patristic era, their real test of doctrine would be the catholicism of the medieval church or of the Tridentine or contemporary Roman Catholic Church and they would use their patristic learning to support this standard, rather than the standard of the Reformation settlement. Newman, in Tract 90, concentrated especially on the articles that deal with the Eucharist, and it is around eucharistic doctrine that the battle would rage for more than a hundred years. A similar sign of where Tractarian sympathies really lay was the essay of Robert Wilberforce in 1843 (the year before his conversion to Roman Catholicism) arguing that transubstantiation properly understood was compatible with the 39 Articles.

It is important that we notice what has happened here. The eucharistic theology of the Scottish-American rite is a synthesis of the sacramental doctrine of John Calvin and Eastern Orthodoxy. This synthesis had provided a way to transcend the restrictive framework of the Reformation controversies over the eucharistic presence and the eucharistic sacrifice. For this reason, there was a measure of common ground for high-church and evangelical eucharistic doctrine. When the parameters of the debate shifted back to the philosophical and theological framework of the West in the Era of the Reformation, the common ground largely vanished. In the terms chosen for the debate, Catholic and Protestant

CHAPTER THREE:

doctrines are basically irreconcilable, and the result was a bitter and growing partisanship that has only recently begun to abate. It is instructive also to note that the American eucharistic prayer does not really lend itself to interpretation along Western Catholic lines . . . so that the debate was carried out oblivious to the theological content of the text which it was meant to interpret.

The doctrinal issue came to a head in the American church in 1843, when Arthur Carey, a graduate of General Seminary, was ordained by Bishop Benjamin Onderdonk. Carey's original examiners had discovered that, as a result of the study of Tract 90, he would not disavow the Tridentine eucharistic doctrine. In order to ordain him, Bishop Onderdonk reconstituted the committee of examiners before proceeding with the ordination. Two prominent New York rectors, nonetheless, appeared at the service to protest Carey's ordination. A furor erupted. An inquiry was conducted into the teaching of the faculty at General Seminary. Although the seminary's reputation suffered for some years, the faculty escaped any disciplinary action. Bishop Onderdonk was not so fortunate. He had made bitter enemies of the Evangelicals, and they finally succeeded in suspending him from his ministry on charges of immoral conduct.[1]

In America as in England, it was the doctrinal stance of the Tractarians rather than their liturgical program that first caught people's attention, as we have seen. Massey Shepherd notes the early goals of the Tractarians with approval. They were:

> . . .nothing less than the restoration to the Church of the full observance of the liturgy as laid out in the Prayer Book: the daily performance of the offices of Morning and Evening Prayer, the celebration of the Holy Communion in addition on all Sundays and holy days, the public administration of the occasional sacraments and rites, and the due observance of the feasts and fasts of the Christian Year in their entirety.[2]

This liturgical emphasis was unsettling to the Evangelicals, who disliked what they considered a disproportionate emphasis on the sacraments, but it was not remarkably different from American high-church tradition of the day. The Catholic affinities and sympathies of the Tractarians meant, however, that they failed to argue the case for the normative character of the Sunday Eucharist (and other parts of their liturgical agenda) on the basis of Reformation principles as well as that of Catholic tradition. There is ample Protestant basis (in the works of Calvin, the Augsburg Confession, the 1552 Prayer Book, and the teaching of the Wesleys) for the sacramental practice which the Tractarians advocated; by failing to ground their program in the Reformation as well as in the Catholic tradition, the Tractarians gave their liturgical program a partisan nature which it need not have had.

Though they did not, in fact, succeed in persuading the Church to implement their early liturgical agenda, their goals were solidly rooted in the Book of Common Prayer and Anglican liturgical tradition. For this reason, though these goals might be resisted, they could hardly be labeled "un-Anglican." At the beginning, the Tractarians manifested no intention of either significant changes in the ceremonial style of eucharistic celebration or revision of liturgical texts. But tractarian sacramental doctrine by its very nature cried out for expression in the outward forms of worship, and the disciples of the Oxford Reformers soon moved beyond the limits set by the early Tractarians in their liturgical agenda, just as after Tract 90 they moved beyond the doctrinal position of the Via Media.

It was, in fact, in the esthetics of worship rather than in doctrinal formulation that the Tractarians were to achieve their greatest success and to effect the greatest changes in the life of the Church in both England and the United States. The Romantic Movement which began toward the end of the eighteenth century prepared the way for all of this. As the Age of the Enlightenment drew to a close, a wave of nostalgia for the Middle Ages engulfed the rationalism which had been the predominant school of thought in the Western world. The Reformation, the Renaissance, and the Enlightenment had looked on the Middle Ages as a time of darkness and decline and had sought their standards in either the early centuries of the church's life or in the "Golden Age" of Greek and Roman classicism. Now, after the tumults of a revolutionary era and the emotional sterility of the prevailing rationalism, the Middle Ages exerted a fascination as the "ages of faith."

Romanticism is evident in much of the culture of the time. The literature of the age was captivated by the Middle Ages, as is manifest in the popularity of the novels of Sir Walter Scott. In architecture, medieval styles became popular first for homes and mansions. Fonthill Abbey and Strawberry Hill, two famous English country houses in this style, reveal the eighteenth-century fashion for the medieval in its more fanciful forms. In a similar way the style would be adapted for public buildings, such as the Houses of Parliament and even railroad stations. It is not surprising, then, that Christians would be led to consider medieval styles (especially pointed Gothic) as the only really appropriate architecture for church buildings. At first, this meant adapting Gothic features to what were basically "one-room" auditory churches. In the United States, Trinity Church in New Haven, Connecticut (1815), and Christ Church Cathedral in Hartford, Connecticut (1828), are surviving examples of this trend (though both have undergone significant subsequent alteration, acquiring chancels). But a more consistent use of medieval architecture for this purpose was not long in coming. Augustus Welby Pugin (1812–1852) was the first articulate spokesman for a more authentic use of Gothic architecture.

It is the Cambridge Camden Society, known as the Ecclesiologists from the name of their monthly magazine, who had the greatest impact, however. John Mason Neale and Benjamin Webb founded this society in 1839 with the stated purpose of promoting "the study of Ecclesiastical Architecture and Antiquities, and the restoration of mutilated Architectural remains." Its goals were not antiquarian, however: it aimed at restoring the Gothic ideal as the norm for buildings used for Christian worship. By 1843 it enjoyed the patronage of two archbishops and sixteen bishops in the Church of England. Similar societies were formed elsewhere with the same goals—in New York, for example, in this country.

The principles of the society were grounded in a highly artificial architectural symbolism, inspired in large part by Durandus of Mende (1230–1296), whose medieval treatise on symbolism became the Bible of the movement. In reality, medieval architecture cannot be made to fit the intricate schemas of this treatise; as a result, Gothic revivalists had a very narrow understanding of the architecture they were promoting, and actually destroyed enormous amounts of genuine medieval work in their "restorations" of medieval English churches. In a similar way, on the American scene, churches built in other styles were redesigned to conform to ecclesiological principles in a manner that often destroyed their architectural integrity and their suitability for the liturgical worship for which they were used.

Sir Kenneth Clark, the historian of the Gothic revival, summarizes the achievements of the Ecclesiologists in this way:[3]

> Through them more than through any other agency the Tractarians gained their ultimate victory. For fifty years almost every new Anglican church was built and furnished according to their instructions, that is to say, in a manner opposed to utility, economy or good sense—a very wonderful achievement in the mid-nineteenth century.

CHAPTER THREE:

What is involved here is not merely a matter of style. A change in style would not in and of itself constitute an architectural revolution. Two factors are involved in the revolutionary character of the achievement of the Ecclesiologists. The first is a change in the dominant aim in the design of churches. Since the Reformation, churches had been designed or redesigned to serve as an appropriate setting for the liturgical requirements of the Book of Common Prayer. Function determined the form which the buildings took. Now the dominant aim in the design of churches became the creation of a numinous space which would foster a sense of mystery, wonder, and awe and give visible expression to "the beauty of holiness." What captivated the Ecclesiologists were the long vistas—the vision of the altar far off seen down the length of a long nave and a long chancel.

The second factor in this architectural revolution is a result of the first. The Ecclesiologists wanted to set Prayer Book worship in the context of medieval churches as they understood them. At first, Anglicans had worked with "two-room" spaces, using the nave as a space for clergy and people to gather for the Proclamation of the Word of God and the chancel as a space for them to gather for the Celebration of the Holy Communion. Later, "one-room" plans predominated in Anglican architectural design. The chancel effectively disappeared as a space separate from the nave, and altar, reading desk, and pulpit were arranged in appropriate ways so that the nave could be used for both parts of the service.

The Ecclesiologists changed all of this. They returned to the "two-room" plan but used it quite differently from the way that it had been used for Anglican worship in the past or even in the worship of the pre-Reformation church. Between nave and altar they reinserted the chancel, which they believed should be a third the length of the church, using cathedral and collegiate churches as their model, even for parish churches. They attempted to integrate chancel and nave into a unified space for worship, so that they favored open rather than solid screens to separate nave and chancel. They generally preferred, however, to demarcate the transition from nave to chancel (and from chancel to altar area) by the use of steps rather than screens. Clergy seating was no longer provided by the reading desk; now clergy were seated in the chancel stalls for the office, and in sedilia to the side of the altar for the Eucharist. For reading the lessons, the Ecclesiologists preferred a lectern in the nave to one side; often this was brought forward, however, to the front of the chancel platform on the side. In a similar way, they preferred pulpits in the nave on the side opposite the lectern, but often the pulpit came to be placed on the front of the chancel platform on the side opposite to the lectern. This design often presented nearly insurmountable problems in terms of acoustics and sight lines, however esthetically attractive it might be.

Initially, the chancel was designated for clergy seating for the office, and the gallery was retained for the singers. Soon, however, the Ecclesiologists came to oppose choir galleries, and to place the singers (vested in surplices) in the chancel. This change in the placement of singers represents a real revolution in church architecture. In the Middle Ages, choirs had been placed in the chancel in cathedral and collegiate churches, but these choirs were in fact *the congregation* of these churches gathered for corporate worship. They were, for the most part, canons and other clergy, members of religious orders, and students at schools attached to these churches. Apart from them, cathedral and collegiate churches had no regular congregations. On special occasions, other people might congregate in such churches for worship, but nave altars or side altars, not the high altar in the choir, would generally be used for such purposes.

CHAPTER THREE:

Much the same rationale obtained after the Reformation in cathedrals and collegiate churches, where the canons or prebendaries, choral vicars, and lay choristers constituted the basic congregation for daily worship. Others might attend daily services; when they did, they too were generally seated in the choir. For larger services, the nave would be used.

In parish churches, such choristers as there were before the Reformation were frequently placed on the rood loft rather than the chancel. The placement of the choir in the chancel, therefore, represents not so much a return to medieval usage as a real innovation in church design, surprising as that may seem.

Leeds Parish Church was the first place where a surpliced choir was placed in the new position, and it became the prototype for subsequent Anglican parish churches. It was erected by its vicar, Walter Hook, to provide for the daily choral offices which his congregation requested and was dedicated in 1841. Its design follows the suggestions of Hook's friend, John Jebb, for whom the architecture of the English cathedral (with the medieval screens removed) constituted the ideal design for parochial worship. However, Jebb used this design in a way that it had not customarily been used, for in cathedrals lay worshipers were customarily seated with the choristers in the chancel, and in parish churches the chancel was not used for choristers. Once Leeds Parish Church had been built, cathedrals and parish churches alike followed its lead, although cathedrals eventually tended to revert to the use of the chancel and the nave, each with its own altar, as alternative spaces for worship, depending on the size of the congregation and the nature of the service. In the parish church, Jebb's theory could be made to work (though it created liturgical problems); in cathedrals it really could not. Contrast earlier figures in the appendix of schematic architectural plans with the plan given there for the typical Gothic revival church.

Perhaps the most welcome achievement of the Ecclesiologists was the removal of the overgrowth of box pews in churches. In some cases these pews had become almost private apartments ("parlor pews"); in many others, pews broke up the space in such a way that other architectural elements were overwhelmed. The reason for the enormous height of some eighteenth-century pulpits was the height of the pew enclosures. From the time of the Gothic revival, churches began to return to the use of slip pews of the kind to which we are accustomed, or the chairs of the kind now customary in many cathedrals. With this change, the major visual foci of the church—table, lectern, pulpit, and font regained their architectural prominence.

Once churches had been laid out according to the Ecclesiologists' idea of Gothic design, the next step was to ornament and furnish them in a similar medieval fashion. The English Reformers had generally removed the rood or crucifix, much of the statuary, shrines, stone altars, crosses and candles, and other ornaments from churches. Walls had been whitewashed (covering medieval paintings). Some stained glass was removed, though much survived. The standard decoration was the table of the commandments flanked by the Apostles' Creed and the Lord's Prayer, usually erected behind the table, and the royal arms, often erected in the place of the rood that had been removed. Puritans were iconoclastic in the theological sense (opposed to the use of representational art in the church), but they never entirely succeeded in imposing their views on the Church as a whole. Modest use of art in symbols carved into the fabric or in the form of paintings behind the altar, as well as occasional statuary (such as Cosin's angels at Durham, to which Peter Smart took violent exception) continued in the Church of England. Cross or even crucifix and candlesticks could be found in the Chapel Royal in some periods and in churches and chapels furnished by some Laudians, though this usage had almost entirely disappeared by the nineteenth century.

With the Gothic revival, all the customary medieval art returned. Some of it met with fierce opposition. Crosses, crucifixes, and candlesticks were matters of controversy. The ceremonial use of incense (although not completely unknown after the Reformation), reservation of the sacrament (for the sick but also sometimes for an extra-liturgical cult of the consecrated species), and the use of the "Sanctus bell" were also offensive to many. In England, they all became matters for complicated legal proceedings. Except for the crucifix, however, Gothic ornament became increasingly common by the end of the nineteenth century. In a similar way, processional cross and torches, and vested acolytes to carry them and assist in the service in other ways, roused heated opposition initially and then gradually became nearly universal.

The use of the sequence of liturgical colors and of vestments underwent a similar development. Since the Reformation, hangings for the altar (and sometimes the pulpit) had customarily been all-purpose. Now color sequences began to be adopted for seasons and holy days, following pre-Reformation English—or, more commonly, especially in the United States—modern Roman Catholic usage.

After the Reformation, only the clergy (and at times the parish clerk) had worn vestments—generally the full-length surplice over the cassock (with tippet for ordained clergy and hoods for those with degrees). With the passage of time, many clergy came to wear only the full-length surplice over street clothes. Only in cathedral and collegiate churches had choirs customarily been vested in surplice. There are occasional exceptions where boys' choirs were formed on the cathedral model—St. Michael's Church in Charleston, South Carolina, had a vested boys' choir at the end of the eighteenth century. Now the cathedral choir in the chancel became a model for parish churches as well (as we have seen in the case of the Leeds Parish Church) and they were vested in surplices. Initially, this innovation roused heated opposition: Bishop McIlvaine of Ohio, a militant Evangelical, put one of his clergy on trial (unsuccessfully) for the introduction of a vested choir. In the course of the century, however, a vested choir became standard with all schools of churchmanship.

The use of colored stoles (generally unknown since 1552) and chalice veil and burse (a post-Reformation Roman Catholic usage) were at first controversial but eventually became almost universal. Full eucharistic vestments and copes first began to come into use in the mid-nineteenth century. They long remained a badge of churchmanship and wearing them has never become universal, though by mid-twentieth century their use was becoming widespread and less controversial. A compromise usage was white linen chasubles with colored stoles—a "broad-church" custom. American Episcopalians generally preferred the Gothic style of chasuble, though some ardent Anglo-Catholics adopted the "fiddle-back" (named for the shape of its back: the sides were completely cut away, so that the arms were not covered) common at the time among Roman Catholics. The use of a cope as a eucharistic vestment (mentioned in the 1549 rubrics and required by Archbishop Parker's advertisements in cathedral and collegiate churches in the reign of Elizabeth I) was frequent in England but uncommon in the United States, where the cope, when used, was sometimes worn for processions, weddings, and baptisms, and also as an episcopal vestment with the miter.

A further adjunct to this return to medieval architecture, ornament, and vestments was the desire to recover medieval ceremonial in worship as well—to make Prayer Book worship "look medieval." In terms of ceremonial, Tractarians came increasingly with passing decades to approximate the usage of the pre-Reformation or the contemporary "Western Rite" in one form or another and to superimpose it on the Book of Common Prayer. In general, the Episcopal Eucharist began to resemble to a greater or lesser extent the style of celebration customary in the Roman Rite. Though at first the Evangelicals bitterly resisted this, in the end they too came to adopt some of the ceremonial usages of this rite. In the end, no school of churchmanship retained the usages common in the early nineteenth century by the end of that century. Massey Shepherd writes,[4] "there is hardly an Episcopalian alive today who is not a ritualist according to the definition of the word a century ago." At its minimum, the changes that took place in the style of celebration entailed the following customs:

1. The gradual abandonment of north-end celebrations for eastward celebrations. North-end celebrations were a liturgical curiosity that made little sense once the altar was moved back against the chancel wall. While a position for the celebrant behind a freestanding altar would accomplish the same purposes, such a position did not generally come into use, and although some evangelical parishes adopted such an arrangement eventually, it was the liturgical movement of the mid-twentieth century that would eventually make this custom popular.

2. The custom of presiding at Ante-Communion from the altar rather than the reading desk.

3. Recovery of a greater use of manual acts by the celebrant.

4. Gradual (and unfortunate) abandonment of the lectern and pulpit (which replaced the reading desk) for the lessons at the Eucharist (which were commonly read from the altar rather than from the places which were designed for reading them).

In greater detail, the standard of ceremonial usage varied. What came to be known as the "Sarum Rite" set as a standard the pre-Reformation English usage as modified by subsequent rubric and canon. This usage gradually took systematic shape during the nineteenth century and reached its full form in the twentieth century in the scholarly publications of the Alcuin Club and in Percy Dearmer's *Parson's Handbook.* In its fullness, it became much more common in England than in the United States, where it seemed quaintly British. Nonetheless, it represented an approach to ceremonial which was congenial to Episcopalians.

"Western Rite" advocates took as their standard the Roman Missal. The process of incorporating liturgical texts and ceremonial usage which conformed the Prayer Book to the Roman Rite developed over the course of the nineteenth century, reaching its final form after the 1928 revision of the American Prayer Book. The stages are marked by the various liturgical guides issued to accomplish this (descriptions of the English works are summarized from Kenneth Stevenson's *Eucharist and Offering*):

> *Directorium Anglicanum* (1858): directions for provision of vestments and furnishings; rubrical interpretations; extensive quotations and supplementary prayers from various sources; conclusion of the Roman canon.

> *The Priest to the Altar* (1861): seasonal secrets, postcommunions, and blessings; 1549, Scottish, and American rites (without expansion); various offertory prayers; portions of the Roman post-Sanctus or epiclesis from the *Apostolic Constitutions;* portions of the conclusion of the Roman canon or 1549 anamnesis; 1662 prayer of oblation after communion; modest concern with ceremonial externals.

> Orby Shipley, *The Ritual of the Altar* (1870): full use of Roman offertory prayers and canon (with the 1662 Prayer of Consecration for the institution narrative).

American Missal (based on 1928 American Book of Common Prayer): the Prayer Book rite supplemented with propers and other material from the Roman Missal; the American eucharistic prayer intact with Roman Rubrics superimposed.

Ritual Notes (for use with 1928 Book of Common Prayer): detailed rubrical direction for celebration according to the Roman Rite.

St Augustine's Prayer Book: devotional manual for American laity with the 1928 Eucharist with Roman additions (no propers).

Although the rubrics can be interpreted in such a way as to make this adaptation of the Prayer Book to the Roman Missal legal in the majority of its details, and although the full eucharistic prayer makes the American Rite easier to use in this way than the English Rite of 1662, the superimposition of Roman Rubrics on the American eucharistic prayer produces a certain theological incoherence, since the structure and the logic of this prayer is different from that of the Roman canon. In the Roman canon, the "words of institution", as that prayer has generally been interpreted, have consecratory force; the logic of the American Prayer places the consecratory force on the invocation. The manual acts of the Roman Rite, as joined to the American eucharistic prayer in the Anglo-Catholic tradition, simply do not fit.

A more common usage than either of the above was that of "Prayer Book Catholics," who followed the ceremonial tradition of the Roman Rite but used the Prayer Book as their altar book, sometimes supplementing it with the rubrically permissible use of the traditional introit, gradual and alleluia verse, offertory, and communion as anthems. Episcopalians in general were attracted to the stately and ceremonious, but doctrinally neutral, usage of English cathedrals.

The Book of Common Prayer 1892

Apart from their gradually disappearing attachment to north-end celebrations and their preference for the outstretched hand as a gesture of blessing and absolution, the Evangelicals cannot be said to have developed a ceremonial style of their own. Instead, they adopted such parts of the Catholic style as they did not find, at any given moment, offensive to them. In this way they gradually adopted the eastward position for the celebrant, the use of colored stoles, altar crosses and candles, vested choirs and acolytes, processional torches and crosses, and processions. They were far more likely than high-churchmen to make use of flags in procession and for decoration. As is true of American Protestants as a whole, they came to make the offering of alms a ceremony in its own right—oblivious to the way in which this ceremonial innovation contradicts the doctrine of justification by grace and savors of Pelagianism. Perhaps the major part of their liturgical energies went into opposition to such Anglo-Catholic ceremonial usages as they found offensive and a paradoxical effort, without real basis in the Reformation itself, to find theological justification for *not* celebrating the Eucharist as the principal act of worship on Sunday.

Throughout the nineteenth century and well into the twentieth controversies raged over ceremonial practices. In England, litigation over such matters reached the courts. In the United States, the controversy reached a climax in attempts to regulate ceremonial usage by canonical legislation. A canon adopted in 1874 forbade the elevation of the eucharistic species or acts of adoration to them. It proved ineffective, however, and was eventually withdrawn.

A final aspect of the Tractarian transformation of worship is to be found in the area of music. The musical rendition of the Kyrie, Gloria in excelsis, and (dialogue, preface,) Sanctus is a significant recovery for the whole church and the Tractarians deserve much, if not most, of the credit for it. Musical rendition of other parts of the Eucharist (the lessons, the Creed, and prayers) remain to some extent a matter of churchmanship today, but the musical tradition for the "ordinary" of the rite has been restored. The use of plainsong rather than harmonized chant remains a Catholic characteristic, but does not arouse general opposition.

Psalmody at the Eucharist is another tractarian emphasis. Plainsong rendition of psalmody for introit, gradual, alleluia verse, offertory, and communion was borrowed by Tractarians from Roman (or Sarum) tradition. Use of some or all of these has commended itself to various schools of high- or Catholic-churchmanship; and the 1979 Prayer Book made the gradual psalm an integral part of the propers.

The most notable Tractarian contribution to the music of the church was in hymnody, however. In the nineteenth century a collection of hymns from various sources had begun to displace metrical psalmody in Episcopal worship. It is from the English Tractarians that the greatest initial enrichment of hymnody was to come. A great body of Latin hymnody was translated into English and made available for worship. John Mason Neale was the most prolific of the translators, as a glance at the list of authors and translators in the Hymnal will reveal. Neale was also a scholar of the Eastern liturgies, and his skillful metrical paraphrases of some of the rich treasury of Eastern prose hymnody enriched our English repertoire of hymns. Perhaps best known are his paraphrases of centos of troparia or refrains for the Song of Moses, "The Day of Resurrection," and "Come, ye faithful, raise the strain."

Lutheran hymnody was also translated and enriched the music of the Episcopal Church. This was an age of hymn-writers as well, and while some of their work now seems sentimental or dated, much that is worthwhile has lasted. Seasonal and festal hymnody enriched the observance of the Church Year, and English versions of Latin eucharistic hymns as well as original compositions had enormous impact on the eucharistic piety and theology of Episcopalians of all schools of churchmanship. The great English collection was *Hymns Ancient and Modern* (1860); in 1868 General Convention permitted bishops to license its use. The Hymnal adopted by the Episcopal Church in 1871 (slightly revised in 1874) was substantially modeled on that English book. The 1871 book contained 520 hymns; it now included some of the metrical psalms and was no longer bound up with the Prayer Book. By now, the metrical psalter, reduced in 1832 to 124 texts, had largely fallen into disuse. The Convention concerned itself only with texts; printers who were licensed to publish it issued their own musical editions. It was not until the twentieth century that the Church would officially regulate hymn tunes or service music.

The Tractarian emphasis on music also led to a greater emphasis on choirs. Choirs of men and boys, on the model of the English cathedrals, became widespread in this period. Mixed choirs also were common. Various models were followed. Some choirs of men and boys were paid; others were volunteer. Mixed choirs might also be paid, or have paid section leaders; others were entirely volunteer.

Children's choirs of various kinds were also established, and parishes with choirs of men and boys might also have girls' choirs. As noted earlier, it became customary to vest choirs and to place them in the chancel. Organs would become the predominant instrument to accompany singing and the tradition of the parish band died out.

The Tractarians achieved their greatest success in fostering more frequent celebration and reception of Communion. They are responsible for the nearly universal custom of an early celebration every Sunday in parishes of every school of churchmanship. It is also not unusual to find a daily celebration of the Eucharist in urban parishes of evangelical or low-church outlook as well as more Catholic parishes. But they achieved this success through an appeal to personal piety and individual conviction—with the result that a sense of the Eucharist as the corporate worship of the church was lost sight of.

The later Sunday service, the principal service in a parish church, often took a theologically unjustifiable form in parishes. Low-church parishes with choral Morning Prayer and sermon were sacramentally impoverished. The Anglo-Catholic preference for a fasting reception of Communion meant that Anglo-Catholic parishes too often had a principal service with few communions—a solemn mass where most of the congregation did not receive. Perversely, some Anglo-Catholics adopted this as an ideal—which led to a rubric in the 1892 Book of Common Prayer requiring that adequate opportunity be given for the congregation to communicate at a celebration. It is true that the Episcopal Church at the present day seems on the threshold of recovering a comprehensive service of word and sacrament as the principal act of Christian worship on the Lord's Day, but that is the result of the Liturgical Movement, not the Tractarians.

William Augustus Muhlenberg, the Memorial Movement, and the Resolution of 1856

To the Prayer Book of 1789 the Episcopal Church over the years added other materials—the Ordinal (1792), the rite for the consecration of a church (1799), and the office for the institution of ministers (1804, revised in 1808 and 1844). There was little interest in revision of the Prayer Book itself for most of the nineteenth century, however. Each party was satisfied to use the existing text of the Prayer Book in its own way, and fearful that revision might alter the status quo to its own disadvantage. The most articulate advocate of revision was William Augustus Muhlenberg, a prophet whom no party could claim. He had come into the Episcopal Church from a Lutheran background and entered its ministry under the sponsorship of Bishop White.

Boone Porter characterizes this remarkable man in this way:[5]

> More than most of his contemporaries, he saw that the pastoral and missionary opportunities of America called for more flexible rubrics. Highly critical of the threadbare routine of early nineteenth-century Anglican worship, he urged a more dramatic and colorful observance of the church year, more and better music, and a fuller use of visual and architectural symbolism. . . . He saw liturgical practices of earlier ages and other churches as resources to be drawn upon when it was advantageous, not as standards to be adopted for their own sake. Deeply as he was concerned over the beauty and transcendent character of worship, he was no less interested in its educational and pastoral impact.

It was this last characteristic which distinguished Muhlenberg from the Tractarians in his liturgical agenda, which in many ways closely resembled theirs and which he implemented on his own very effectively. He administered the Eucharist weekly at the Parish of the Holy Communion in New York. Instrumental in the preparation of the Prayer Book Collection of Hymns in 1826, he made use of a wide variety of music and introduced a vested choir to sing the psalms. He made effective and imaginative use of Gothic architecture in the building of this church.

Yet, although at first attracted by the Tractarians, he was doctrinally unsympathetic to their aims; he even disclaimed the label of "high churchman" which in many ways was appropriate for him. He was to testify that, upon reading Newman's *Development of Doctrine*,[6] "I flew back, not to rest on the pier of High Churchism from which this bridge of Puseyism springs, but on the solid rock of Evangelical truth, as republished by the Reformers."

In 1853 the famous "Muhlenberg Memorial" went before

CHAPTER THREE:

General Convention. Massey Shepherd summarizes this remarkable document as follows:[7]

> It dealt with three basic topics, each of them closely interwoven—Evangelism, Liturgy, and Church Unity. The underlying concern was the lack of effective response to the treasures of the Episcopal Church's faith, worship, and order, on the part of both Christians and pagans in the increasingly varied classes of American society. The Memorial questions whether "the traditional customs and usages" of the Episcopal Church were any longer "competent to the task of preaching and dispensing the Gospel to all sorts and conditions of men, and so, adequate to do the work of the Lord in this land and in this age."

The meager immediate result, in terms of liturgy, was the permission to use Morning Prayer, the Litany, and the Eucharist as separate services on Sunday morning, granted by a resolution of the House of Bishops in the Convention of 1856. The long-term result of the Memorial Movement, however, was to lessen the bitterness of party strife in the church, and to create a position between the two parties—the "broad church" (heir in this to Latitudinarians, though very different in other respects).

It is important to look for a moment at what the permission to separate the "accumulated" services meant to the liturgical life of the church. It permitted the separation of services which did not fit together well as a continuous and integrated whole. However, it also fragmented in ways that had not been foreseen the wholeness of Sunday worship as a comprehensive service of word and sacrament in the life of a parish. The increasing popularity of "early Communion" meant that parish congregations no longer worshiped together week by week, but chose what service they would attend on Sunday morning as a matter of personal preference.

Those who attended an early communion were almost never exposed to the psalms or the Old Testament, seldom heard a sermon, prayed only for the church (not the world), and took part in a rite which focused heavily on the Atonement, but paid little attention to the doctrines of Creation and the Incarnation. Those who attended a later service of Morning Prayer heard psalms and both Old and New Testament, prayed (if the Litany was used) for the church and the world, had their attention focused on creation (the Venite and Benedicite) and the Incarnation (the Te Deum and Benedictus Dominus), but were little exposed to the proclamation of Christ's saving death (the Atonement), and did not participate in the Eucharist, the intended climax of Sunday worship. In this same period, baptism began to be celebrated more and more as a semiprivate family rite, no longer integrated into Morning (or Evening) Prayer.

William Reed Huntington
and the Book Annexed of 1883

Toward the end of the century, William Reed Huntington took up the work of William Augustus Muhlenberg. Like Muhlenberg, he was someone whom no school of churchmanship could claim. While Muhlenberg was a prophet and a visionary, Huntington was a scholar and a statesman. His ruling passion was the cause of Church Unity (a concern which he shared with Muhlenberg) and his monument is the Chicago-Lambeth Quadrilateral, whose principles he first outlined in a sermon in 1870. Massey Shepherd writes of him,[8] "No Ritualist on either side of the Atlantic could match Huntington's knowledge of the bibliography of liturgics. . . . His concern was for the basic principles and rationale of the liturgy, and to this he added a sureness of taste."

Any prospect of Prayer Book revision faltered in the 1870s. Doctrinal and liturgical controversy gave birth to the Reformed

Episcopal Church, a schismatic group which broke off over the doctrine of baptismal regeneration in 1873, and to the Ritual Canon of 1874, which sought to restrict tractarian ceremonial practices. But by 1880 Huntington was able to successfully introduce a resolution creating a joint committee of General Convention to examine whether revision should be undertaken. This committee produced in 1883 the *Book Annexed.* This book represented a concern for flexibility and enrichment. It proposed one new feast, the restoration of the Gospel canticles to Evening Prayer and the remaining verses of the Benedictus Dominus Deus to Morning Prayer, provisions for shortening the offices on weekdays and the Eucharist on Sundays, and some new offices and occasional prayers.

Favorably received in 1883, the book met with a hostile response in ensuing years. When a new committee was formed in 1886, Huntington declined to serve on it, feeling that he would be a more effective advocate on the floor of Convention without ties to the committee proposing revisions. The ultimate result was the Prayer Book of 1892, to which we will turn in the final section of this chapter. This book incorporated some of the modest proposals for revision from the *Book Annexed,* but omitted much of the new material in that book.

The Sunday Service in the Prayer Book of 1892

An outline of the Sunday service as revised in 1892 follows. Note that the rubrics of the book now incorporate the provisions of the 1856 Resolution permitting the separation of the component rites. The outline will focus primarily on the Eucharist, which now came more and more to be celebrated without the other two rites.

The Proclamation of the Word of God

Morning Prayer (optional)
  Confession optional if Communion office follows.
  Collect of day omitted if Communion office follows.
Litany (optional)
Ante-Communion
  Lord's Prayer without doxology (optional when Morning
      Prayer precedes)
  Collect for Purity
  Decalogue (at least once a Sunday) and/or Summary of the
      Law
  Threefold Kyrie (if decalogue is not used)
  Decalogue collect (optional)
  Collect of the Day
  Epistle
  Gospel
  Nicene Creed (printed in text) or Apostles' Creed (if not
      used in Morning Prayer)
  Sermon

The Celebration of the Holy Communion

  Offertory Sentences
  Collection of Alms
  Presentation of Alms (hymn or anthem allowed)
  Preparation and Placement of Bread and Wine on the Altar
  Prayer for the Whole State of Christ's Church Militant
  Exhortation (required once a month)
  Invitation, Confession, Absolution, Comfortable Words
  Sursum Corda and Preface
  Sanctus (detached from last part of Preface)
  Prayer of Humble Access
  Prayer of Consecration

Hymn and communion
  (rubric requiring opportunity for congregation to com-
    municate)
Lord's Prayer
Postcommunion prayer
Gloria in excelsis or hymn
Blessing

The changes in the Eucharist represent modest attempts to provide a shorter service. The initial Lord's Prayer, when used, is now
recited without doxology. The Decalogue now need be used only
once a Sunday; the Exhortation, only once a month. Since a Creed
was used at the Eucharist when it was separated from Morning
Prayer, the Nicene Creed was now printed in the text of the rite
(though on most occasions the Apostles' Creed could be used as
an alternative). The rubrics now allow a hymn or anthem when
the alms are presented. The last two offertory sentences (new to
the American book) may perhaps be meant to serve the same
purpose, as in the Scottish rite, but the rubrics do not distinguish
them from the other sentences. The Sanctus has been detached
from the last part of the preface, so that the people join in reciting
only it, rather than the last part of the preface as well. The controversies of the day led to the insertion of the rubric requiring that
adequate opportunity be given to the congregation to receive
communion.

The resulting rite does not really differ significantly from that
of 1789. Although, as we noted above, there is a loss when it is
separated from Morning Prayer and the Litany, the Eucharist is a
separate rite with its own distinct beginning, and the juncture of
the two rites is awkward. The abbreviations in the service involve
elements added at the Reformation—the decalogue and the exhortation—that are intrusions on the classic structure of the rite.
In coming years they will be used less and less frequently: the

rubrics in 1892 are recognition of a process which will continue until these elements disappear almost entirely from regular use.

Musical provisions continued trends noted earlier in this chapter. By 1892 the number of texts in the hymnal had reached 679; this hymnal, like that of 1871/1874, was issued in musical editions by the publishers licensed to print it. Finally, in 1916 a hymnal (with 561 hymns) was authorized by Convention with its own tunes. It is only with this last hymnal that the Church itself took responsibility for publishing either authorized hymn tunes or authorized service music.

Notes to Chapter Three

BIBLIOGRAPHIC NOTES

The text of the 1892 eucharistic rite can be most easily studied by referring to the critical apparatus to the 1928 rite in Bernard Wigan, *The Liturgy in English* (London, Oxford University Press, 1962). Some parishes may still have their altar book for this rite, as the author's does. A summary of revisions can be found in *Prayer Book Studies IV* (New York, Church Pension Fund, 1957).

The period covered by these years is briefly treated in H. Boone Porter's article, "Toward an Unofficial History of Episcopal Worship" in Malcom C. Bursin, editor, *Worship Points the Way* (New York, Seabury, 1981), and at greater length in Massey Shepherd, *The Reform of Liturgical Worship* (New York, Oxford University Press, 1961). Shepherd's book and Porter's article both assess the impact of the Oxford Movement and the Ecclesiologists on Episcopal worship. Robert Bruce Mullin, *Episcopal Vision/American Reality* (New Haven, Yale, 1986) studies the gradual displacement of the older Hobartian high-churchmanship by the Tractarians and their successors. Kenneth Stevenson, *Eucharist and Offering* (New York, Pueblo, 1986) also devotes a chapter to changes in ceremonial and textual "supplementation" to the Prayer Book rite under the impact of the Oxford Movement. Powell Mills Dawley narrates the impact of the Oxford

Movement and the uproar caused by the ordination of Arthur Carey in *The Story of the General Theological Seminary* (New York, Oxford University Press, 1969).

The two "prophets of renewal," William Augustus Muhlenberg and William Reed Huntington, receive extended treatment in Shepherd's book, and Porter briefly assesses their importance in his article. Mullin's book also discusses Muhlenberg's "evangelical catholicism."

The sources listed for the history of church music in the bibliographic notes for the last chapter should be consulted for music in this period as well.

Shepherd's book treats the "architectural revolution" of the Gothic Revival. The standard work on this style is Sir Kenneth Clark, *The Gothic Revival: An Essay in the History of Taste* (Constable, 1950). Another important study is J. F. White, *The Cambridge Movement: the Ecclesiologists and the Gothic Revivalists* (Cambridge, University Press, 1962). The revival is set in the larger context of the history of Anglican architecture in G. W. O. Addleshaw and Frederick Etchells, *The Architectural Setting of Anglican Worship* (London, Faber and Faber, 1948).

NOTES ON THE TEXT

1. Cf. Powell Mills Dawley, *The Story of the General Theological Seminary.* Robert Bruce Mullin also gives an account of the Carey ordination and the Onderdonk trial in *Episcopal Vision/American Reality.* The extent to which the charges against Bishop Onderdonk were justified is still a matter of debate. What is clear is that his suspension was motivated by partisan animosities at the time.

2. Massey Shepherd, *The Reform of Liturgical Worship,* page 18.

3. Sir Kenneth Clark, *The Gothic Revival,* page 238, cited in Shepherd, page 24. As Clark acknowledges, the Ecclesiologists do deserve credit for calling the Church's attention to its neglect of its buildings and summoning it to raise the standards of its worship. The renewed emphasis on the numinous in church architecture must be accounted a gain, even though the often rigid reliance on a narrow reading of Durandus to achieve this wrought considerable mischief.

4. Shepherd, page 17.

5. Boone Porter, "Toward an Unofficial History of Episcopal Worship,' in Malcom C. Bursin, editor, *Worship Points the Way,* pages 101–102.

6. William Augustus Muhlenberg, as quoted in Anne Ayres, *The Life and Work of William Augustus Muhlenberg* (Harper, 1881), cited in Shepherd, page 40.

7. Shepherd, pages 40–41.

8. Shepherd, page 48.

CHAPTER THREE:

The Book of Common Prayer 1928

The 1928 Revision of the Eucharistic Rite

The limited additional flexibility and enrichment of the 1892 Prayer Book proved acceptable to all parties and introduced a modest improvement in the eucharistic rite. Not all of the changes suggested in the *Book Annexed* or in subsequent discussion had been adopted, however, and the new book did not end the call for revision. In 1913 the Diocese of California, with the support of the Diocese of Arizona, presented a memorial to General Convention requesting the formation of a new commission to prepare proposals for further revisions. Edward Lamb Parsons acted as chief spokesman for further revision, and the convention appointed the commission.

Besides Parsons, Howard St. George of Nashotah House, John Wallace Suter, Sr., and Charles Lewis Slattery were the chief architects of the revision which resulted. All except St. George were disciples and admirers of William Reed Huntington, chief spokesman for the 1892 revision. The process took 15 years and moved much more rapidly in the House of Deputies than in the House of Bishops. It was only when Parsons was elected a bishop that revision began to make real headway in the House of Bishops. In the meantime, other matters engaged the church's energies. On the whole, the eucharistic rite was not substantially altered. Many changes were those proposed but not adopted for the 1892 revision; others were similar to changes being considered in proposals for revision elsewhere in the Anglican Communion in the 1920s. In 1925 General Convention decided to halt further proposals for revision so that final approval could be given to a book in 1928. This meant that the 1928 American Book could not take full advantage of all that was being suggested elsewhere in the revisions of the 1920s.

In the final 1928 rite, the rubric requiring a "north-end" position for the celebrant was revised so as to direct the celebrant to stand before the Holy Table, recognizing what was in fact becoming common practice. The initial Lord's Prayer was now made optional at all times. Rubrics now permitted less frequent use of the Decalogue (once a month) and of the Exhortation (three times a year). In actual fact, these two components of the rite fell out of general use altogether in the decades to come. The longer commandments in the Decalogue could now also be used in shorter form. The salutation was added to the Collect of the Day. A response to the conclusion of the Gospel was added for optional use (and came to be almost universally used). A new rubric allowed a hymn or anthem before the Gospel—thus permitting use of either the traditional gradual psalmody or a sequence hymn. The practical effect of these changes was to conform the Ministry of the Word more closely to the 1549 (and medieval Roman) shape.

Particular intercession might be incorporated into the rite in three ways:

1. By use of the Bidding Prayer before the sermon;

2. By use of authorized intercessions before the sermon;

3. By bidding the secret intercession of the congregation before the Prayer for the Whole State of Christ's Church.

These provisions responded to a real need, but the solutions are liturgically awkward. In practice, prayers were often added to the biddings at the offertory, which goes beyond the language of the rubric and leads to a duplication of much intercessory material. The most practical solution, inserting particular names in the petitions of the Prayer for the Whole State of Christ's Church, was not provided for in the rubrics of the 1928 rite and did not become common until later.

In the Celebration of the Holy Communion, the components were adjusted to conform more closely to the Scottish order: the Lord's Prayer was placed before (rather than after) Communion, and the Prayer of Humble Access was removed from its position between the Sanctus and the post-Sanctus and placed immediately before Communion, thus reestablishing the link between two parts of what would be called in 1979 the Great Thanksgiving. The altered position of the Lord's Prayer and the Prayer of Humble Access caused some comment, raising fears on the part of Evangelicals that an interval between the conclusion of the consecration and the reception of Communion would foster adoration of the consecrated species. The celebrant was now directed to "offer" the bread and wine at the offertory, as in the Scottish rite, and provision was made for a hymn or anthem during the offertory (not just during the presentation, as in 1892).

The Gloria in excelsis was not restored to its traditional position in the Ministry of the Word, but its text was restored to its more traditional Western form by removing the extra phrase added in 1552 to incorporate the full Agnus Dei in the canticle.

The principal doctrinal shift was a petition (not just a Thanksgiving) for the departed in the Prayer for the Whole State of Christ's Church. The word "militant" was also dropped from the bidding at this time, since the church militant is normally understood to be restricted to the living and not to include the departed. Petitions for the departed were also added elsewhere in the book.

This disturbed some Evangelicals, but it responded to a real pastoral need, and the petition at the Eucharist was in fact drafted by an Evangelical (the Bishop of Virginia). The period after World War I was not an opportune time to raise objections to prayers for the departed, and the Evangelicals made the mistake of raising the objection first about the prayer for memorial days. In the end, the petition at the Eucharist was adopted, as were other prayers for the departed elsewhere in the book. The petition at the Eucharist is an interesting prayer: unlike traditional Western prayers for "rest and peace," it asks for "continual growth in God's love and service." We should note, as Massey Shepherd does in his commentary on All Saints' Day in the Prayer Book, that no distinction is made, here or elsewhere, between the saints and the rest of the departed. There is therefore no suggestion of the doctrine of purgatory to which the Reformers objected. The petition is doctrinally akin to the patristic theology of Gregory of Nyssa, for whom God's perfection consists in remaining always the same, while human perfection consists in "perpetual growth" (in this life and the next) into God's likeness.

Two revisions, proposed in 1925 but defeated in 1928, were the restoration of the Benedictus qui venit and that of the Agnus Dei. The defeat of the Agnus Dei was largely accidental. From the text of the Benedictus qui venit some of the Anglo-Catholics, in debates on the revision, drew doctrinal conclusions that rendered it unacceptable to other parties in the church, and the Revision Commission itself urged its defeat. The Agnus Dei was later printed with the service music in the 1940 Hymnal for (rubrically permissible) use as a hymn during Communion, and many settings for the Sanctus included music for the Benedictus qui venit, which was added (unrubrically) by those who desired it. Even though it was not printed in the Hymnal, it was available when these settings were issued by other publishers.

CHAPTER FOUR:

The older provisions for shortening Morning Prayer when used with the Eucharist were retained. Besides these, a new rubric (borrowed from the Canadian Book of 1922) allowed Morning Prayer to be terminated after the first lesson and one of the morning canticles. When the 1943 office lectionary was adopted with propers specifically chosen for their relation to the eucharistic lessons, a rite with a comprehensive ministry of the word became possible. It was, unfortunately, not widely used. The older custom of celebrating Morning Prayer with the Eucharist was falling out of use, and it was only the liturgically perceptive who saw the advantages of the new provision. The combined rite which resulted was a great improvement over the older provisions, but it was not a perfect solution, for two reasons:

1. the combined service still had two beginnings—the preces of Morning Prayer and the Collect for Purity of the Eucharist;

2. with the loss of the litany, the intercessions which were part of the rite were still restricted to "the whole state of Christ's Church" and did not include the world at large.

The appropriate musical companion to the Prayer Book of 1928 was the Hymnal of 1940, specifically designed for use with the 1928 rite. It drew on a wide range of English hymnody, and also contained a large number of hymns translated from Latin, Greek, and German sources (a trend which had begun in the mid-nineteenth century). Its service music section provided settings in both plainsong and other styles for the congregational portions of the Eucharist as well as other rites. Additional musical provisions were made in another official publication, the Choral Service Book, which gave directions for singing the portions of the rite normally chanted by the celebrant in Western usage (such as prayers, lessons, and the prefaces to the eucharistic prayer, as well as the introduction to the Lord's Prayer).

The outline which follows shows the shape of the Sunday service in this Prayer Book. While Morning Prayer and the Litany were still both used at times in combination with the Eucharist, all three services were very seldom used together at the same time. It became customary in some parishes to sing the Litany in procession before the Eucharist in Lent and Advent—treating it as an essentially penitential rite.

The Proclamation of the Word of God

Morning Prayer (optional)
  (abbreviated as in earlier Prayer Books *or*
  concluded after the first lesson and canticle)
The Litany (optional)
  (sometimes sung before the Eucharist in Advent and
    Lent)
Ante-Communion
  Lord's Prayer (optional)
  Collect for Purity
  Decalogue (required once a month) and/or Summary of
    the Law
  Threefold Kyrie (required if the Decalogue is omitted)
  Decalogue Collect (optional)
  Salutation and Collect of the Day.
  Epistle
  Hymn or anthem (optional)
  Gospel with responses at announcement and conclusion
  Nicene Creed (or Apostles' Creed)
  Bidding Prayer or authorized intercessions (optional)
  Sermon

The Celebration of the Holy Communion

Offertory Sentences
Offertory hymn or anthem (optional)
Collection of alms
Presentation of alms
Preparation, placement, and offering of bread and wine
Biddings for the secret intercessions of the congregation
Prayer for the Whole State of Christ's Church
Exhortation (optional except three times a year)
Invitation, confession, absolution, and comfortable words
Sursum Corda and Preface
Sanctus
Prayer of Consecration (as in 1789)
Lord's Prayer
Prayer of Humble Access
Hymn or anthem (optional) and Communion
Postcommunion Prayer
Gloria in excelsis or hymn
Blessing

Trends in the Use of the 1928 Rite

The architectural, musical, and ceremonial trends which began in the second third of the nineteenth century continued and reached their final form in the decades after the adoption of the 1928 rite, as we noted in the last chapter. On the whole, the celebration of the Eucharist by all schools of churchmanship came to resemble, to a greater or lesser extent, that customary in the Roman Rite—so much so, that Episcopalians would probably not have believed that the style of celebration in nearly universal use until about 1830 had ever been customary in the church.

With the revisions made in 1928, the rite could be conformed in most of its externals to the Roman rite. Introit, gradual, offertory, and communion anthems from the psalms customary in that rite were all rubrically permissible. Eucharistic vestments could be and were worn with increasing frequency. The sequence of liturgical colors had become customary. Use of acolytes was common. Most parishes scheduled an early celebration on Sundays and usually one or more on weekdays. The eastward position for the celebrant became normal, as did candles and crosses on or behind the altar and vested chancel choirs. Manual acts and similar gestures were in common use. At services with music, at least Kyrie and Sanctus were normally sung, and the Agnus Dei and Gloria in excelsis were commonly sung as well. A sung Sursum Corda and preface was not uncommon.

"Advanced" Anglo-Catholics frequently went beyond the rubrics and conformed the rite ceremonially and textually in most respects to the Roman mass. Proper prayers were often used by Anglo-Catholics at the offertory and postcommunion. Most celebrants used some of the private devotions at various points in the service which were printed in the Roman Missal, or such others as they thought appropriate. The salutation was added where customary in the Roman Mass (before the Gospel, the Sursum Corda, the postcommunion, and the dismissal, which was added by them before the blessing). Many used the Sanctus bell (a gong or set of bells rung at certain times during the eucharistic prayer) and incense. The preparation from the Roman Missal (Psalm 43 with antiphon, confession, suffrages, and collect) was used by some, either in the sacristy or silently or aloud at the altar. Some also added the last Gospel (the first chapter of John, read after the final blessing) and even the so-called "Leonine prayers," authorized by Pope Leo XIII. Other schools of churchmanship added such of these practices as they considered appropriate.

A Morning Prayer parish would generally have Morning Prayer with music and sermon as its late service, with the Communion at this hour one Sunday a month. The various schools of high-churchmen would schedule a sung Eucharist or Solemn Mass for the late service. In places where an older high-church tradition had not been transformed into a predominantly Anglo-Catholic orientation, Morning Prayer and the Eucharist were sometimes scheduled on alternate Sundays at the late service. Many parishes scheduled a service between the early celebration and the late service for church-school families. This took many forms: it might be essentially the same as the later service, it might be a weekly Eucharist (even when this was not customary at the later service), it might be an abbreviated service of some sort. Sometimes children attended the beginning of a service and then went to church-school classes. In other places, an informal "church-school service" was held in a chapel or in the parish house for younger children, while parents and older children attended the service in the church. In short, a bewildering variety of Sunday services was available to the average congregation. At times, the style of churchmanship would vary between one service and another in the same parish.

Theologically, the doctrine of the real presence (but not that of transubstantiation) became common in the Episcopal Church. The logic of the prayer for supplementary consecration would suggest that consecration is effected by (the words of institution and) the invocation, but—influenced by medieval Catholic tradition and by the ceremonial emphasis of the celebrant's manual acts, most Episcopalians would probably have asserted that it was the words of institution which were consecratory. On a popular level, at least, the Scottish doctrinal basis of the prayer had been forgotten. Most Episcopalians would have held the doctrine of the eucharistic sacrifice in some form, but the idea of the Eucharist as a propitiatory sacrifice was generally confined to Anglo-Catholics. Generally, they were far more apt than other Episcopalians to "offer the Eucharist for" particular purposes or intentions. In a similar matter, while most Episcopalians came to consider reverence before Christ's presence in the sacrament appropriate, only Anglo-Catholics favored an extraliturgical cult of sacramental devotions (through groups like the Confraternity of the Blessed Sacrament), such as Benediction, Adoration, and processions with the sacramental species.

Toward Further Revision

As we noted above, extensive liturgical revision was underway elsewhere in the Anglican Communion in the 1920s. In particular, there was considerable ferment in England, where the Church itself produced two revisions only to have both turned down by Parliament, which still held the final authority in the authorization of the Book of Common Prayer. Revision was successfully undertaken in most other parts of the Communion. The constitutional provision in the Episcopal Church that revisions be adopted by two successive conventions, however, limited the impact that these revisions had on the American Book of 1928.

In 1928 the Revisions Committee had originally been given authority to make editorial corrections in the Prayer Book after its adoption in 1928. From 1928 until 1940 it had occupied itself with the creation of a new lectionary for the Daily Office (published after extensive trial use in 1943) and the publication of *The Book of Offices,* a book of supplementary services. In 1940 it was reconstituted and given canonical status as the Standing Liturgical Commission. In 1943 it proposed that General Convention authorize it to prepare a draft revision for study and possible adoption on the 400th anniversary of the Book of Common Prayer in 1949. This request was not granted, and in 1946 it presented a more modest proposal for a series of Prayer Book Studies for the church to consider. General Convention gave its authorization, and over the years to come the Commission issued Prayer Book Studies I–XV. This series included, in Prayer Book Studies IV (1953), a proposed revision of the eucharistic liturgy. We will return to this liturgy later in this chapter. Before doing so, we will turn our attention to the Liturgical Movement, which was beginning to have an increasing impact on the worship of the church.

The beginnings of the Liturgical Movement have been variously dated. In its Roman Catholic form, its initial phase should be dated to the work of Dom Prosper Gueranger, who in the nineteenth century refounded the Benedictine Abbey at Solesmes and sought to restore the Roman Rite to its historical integrity (which meant, for him, its pure medieval form). The focus of this phase of the movement was thus historical research and restoration. The Oxford Movement in the Anglican Communion showed a parallel interest in restoring the worship of the Church to its medieval form as modified by subsequent legislation at the time of the Reformation and by Cranmer's liturgical work. Its norms were generally the 1549 English or the 1637 Scottish Prayer Book and the Sarum Rite. For this stage of the liturgical movement, the Middle Ages were the real norm. This phase may be said to have culminated in Anglicanism in the wave of revision in the 1920s, and its most characteristic representative was Walter Howard Frere, a member of the Community of the Resurrection and Bishop of Truro. He was the primary English spokesman for the English or Sarum usage as an Anglican standard and a leading figure for revision of the English Prayer Book, although he ultimately opposed the book presented to Parliament in 1928.

The phase of the Liturgical Movement which followed was pastoral in its orientation. In its Roman Catholic form, it is often dated from the work of Dom Lambert Beauduin in Belgium, starting in 1909. Similar work was soon undertaken in France, in

Klosterneuburg in Austria, and at Maria Laach in Germany. Pius Parsch of Klosterneuberg was a leading figure in the work in German-speaking countries. The Liturgical Movement in this phase sought to make worship pastorally effective in the lives of contemporary Christians. In its Anglican form, this phase took shape in the Parish and People Movement in England and in the work of Associated Parishes in the United States. The English landmarks are *Liturgy and Society* (1935), written by A. G. Hebert, and *The Parish Communion,* a series of essays edited by him. Hebert was greatly influenced by Pius Parsch and also by the monks of Maria Laach under Dom Idelfons Herwegen (1874–1946), its abbot.

By this time, the Eucharist as the normative form of Sunday worship was beginning to emerge from its partisan association with Anglo-Catholicism and find wider acceptance in Anglicanism. Dean William Palmer Ladd of the Berkeley Divinity School acted as a catalyst in awakening the American church to the Liturgical Movement and in introducing Episcopalians to the work of Hebert and the German Benedictines. Urban Holmes characterizes his approach in this way:[1]

> Ladd's advocacy of liturgical reform had much in common with Hebert, but was filtered through his admiration of the Nonjurors—who he believed understood Cranmer as Laud did not—coupled with the passion for souls of John Wesley. He considered the Sarum use, an anachronism from fifteenth century England, as much to be avoided as the Western Use of the Roman Catholic Counter Reformation.

Like Muhlenberg and Huntington before him, he did not easily fit in any of the current parties or schools of churchmanship. In its day, his curious *obiter dicta* on the liturgy in *Prayer Book Interleaves* (1942) did much to familiarize the church with the Liturgical Movement and to encourage it to ask the right questions about worship. Today, it seems strangely dated in outlook.

Several members of seminary faculties in this period did work on early liturgical texts. Prominent among them were Frank Gavin and Burton Scott Easton of General Seminary, Edward Rochie Hardy of the Berkeley Divinity School, and Cyril Richardson of Union Seminary. Yet none of them was greatly concerned with liturgical revision, and most preferred to celebrate "the Western Rite" according to the usages of the American missal.

Two seminary professors who did take a leading role in the work of revision were Bayard Hale Jones, who taught first at the Church Divinity School of the Pacific and later at the University of the South, and Massey Hamilton Shepherd, who taught at the Church Divinity School of the Pacific for most of his career and also at the summer school for graduate study at the University of the South. Jones and Bishop Parsons were the authors of the first important study of the 1928 American Book of Common Prayer, *The American Prayer Book, Its Origins and Principles* (1937); Shepherd published the definitive study on that book, *The Oxford American Prayer Book Commentary* (1950). Jones belongs to the history of the 1928 Book; Shepherd spans the transition from that book to the 1979 rite.

The Liturgical Movement found its principal voice in this country through the Associated Parishes, which Massey Shepherd helped to found in 1946. Most of its leading members are probably best described as "Prayer Book Catholics" who were influenced by the Liturgical Movement in England and in the Roman Catholic Church, but the organization was never narrowly partisan and its members had various theological backgrounds. This organization worked to make the 1928 Prayer Book an effective instrument of renewal, mission, and outreach. Their tracts (of which *The Parish Eucharist* and *A Parish Program for Liturgy and*

Mission were the most significant) and their conferences (whose papers were published in several collections) were effective tools for educating the grass-roots church in the purposes and principles of the liturgical movement. For the first phase of its existence, its members were "prayer-book fundamentalists." American Episcopalians had to become familiar with the strengths of their 1928 rite before they realized its weaknesses and limitations and sought to move beyond it.

The Rite of Prayer Book Studies IV (1953)

The Eucharistic Liturgy of Prayer Book Studies IV marks in many ways the end of an era in Episcopal worship, although this was far from apparent at the time. The Standing Liturgical Commission in the preface to the rites in this series declares its intentions in the following words:

> The objective we have pursued is the same as that expressed by the Commission for the Revision of 1892: *Resolved,* That this Committee, in all its suggestions and acts, be guided by those principles of liturgical construction and ritual use which have guided the compilation and amendments of the Book of Common Prayer, and have made it what it is.

The rites in this series still attempt to be faithful to these goals; by the time that work began on the revision that was to produce the Book of Common Prayer 1979, it had become apparent that it was no longer possible responsibly to undertake the work of revision within limits so narrowly defined.

The eucharistic rite of Prayer Book Studies IV is reputedly primarily the work of Bayard Hale Jones. Although it proposes significant changes, in retrospect it is clear that the rite is most closely akin to the revisions elsewhere in the Anglican Communion in the 1920s; it does not reveal the impact of the scholarly work which was going on at the time and which was to result in significantly different rites in the future. Although Dom Gregory Dix's *Shape of the Liturgy* had been published in 1945 and was already reaching a wide audience, it had little impact on the "shape" of this rite. Again and again in the rationale found in Part II of Prayer Book Studies IV, an important insight will be stated, but the authors will then retreat from working out the implications and consequences of that insight in the rite which they drafted. Since this rite never went into official use, we will not outline it in full, but comment on its salient features (and failings).

A significant feature of the liturgy is the skillful use of titles and subtitles to set off the sections of the rite. This feature is one which all subsequent revisions would take up, although the particular titles and subtitles would vary somewhat.

Like prior American rites, the 1953 rite makes provision for the use of the eucharistic liturgy with either Morning Prayer or the Litany. The provisions for combining the rite with Morning Prayer do not differ significantly from those in the 1928 Book. The directions for beginning the Eucharist with the litany, however, draw on the suggestions of W. H. Frere in England and resemble those adopted in 1979. The Litany is to conclude with its Kyrie, which in turn becomes the Kyrie of the Eucharist, the preceding portion of the eucharistic rite being omitted. When the Litany is used in this way, the Great Intercession in the Eucharist itself may be shortened to what amounts to an offertory collect. In 1979 the same provisions would be made, except that the Prayers of the People may be altogether omitted when the Litany is used, since the 1979 rite avoids offertory prayers.

Another proposal taken up in the 1979 Book was to form from the initial portion of the rite and the Exhortation "An Office of Preparation," which might be used separately or as the introduction to the rite itself. In its details, the "office" does not seem to have been consistently developed. The authors recognize the Decalogue as essentially a means for the examination of conscience, so that when the office is used separately, it may be concluded with a confession. When it is used with the Eucharist, however, the Confession remains in its 1928 position—with the result that the "examination of conscience" is separated from the confession by the whole of the Ministry of the Word, the offertory, and the Great Intercession. The 1979 Penitential Order brought the confession into the "office" as a normal component; by failing to do so, the 1953 revisers rendered the office essentially pointless as an introduction to the eucharistic rite. The use of the salutation at various points in the rite had become customary among many, as we noted above; the 1953 revisers added it where it seemed to them to make sense: before the Collect for Purity, the Sursum Corda, and the postcommunion. The decision in 1979 was somewhat different, but the principle was established by then that the use of the salutation had no doctrinal meaning worth debating and should be decided on other principles of liturgical structure.

The Ministry of the Word may begin with a hymn or anthem. This provision is given in a rubric in the text of the rite, rather than in the general rubrics, as had been customary before. By this provision the revisers sought to make explicit provision for the traditional psalmody for introit, gradual, offertory, and communion anthems, which were to be published in a separate book. In this portion of the rite, the Gloria in excelsis is finally restored to its 1549 (and traditional Western) position, as in 1979. No provision is made for an Old Testament reading in the Eucharist itself; those who wanted to recover that would still have to do so by using shortened Morning Prayer before the rite. The anomalous position of the Creed, before rather than after the Sermon is noted but justified. The provision for use of the bidding prayer before the sermon is deleted, but "special intercessions" may still be made at this point in the rite, although potentially such intercessions, like the bidding prayer, can duplicate much of the General Intercession which comes later in the rite.

More curious is the failure to "unclutter" the offertory by removing the General Intercession and the Confession. The original position of the General Intercession at the Conclusion of the Ministry of the Word is noted, but treated as only a relic of the era of the catechumenate. The General Intercession printed in the text of the rite is still the Prayer for the Whole State of Christ's Church—the bidding makes no mention of the world and so restricts the scope of the intercession (more, in fact, than the text of the prayer does). A rubric allows the Celebrant either to ask for the secret intercessions of the congregation at this point or to offer authorized prayers (thus legalizing a common practice but potentially duplicating much of the material in the General Intercession). The most reasonable way of dealing with particular intercessions, incorporating them into the General Intercession, is discussed in the rationale but rejected as beyond the abilities of the average celebrant to do correctly. A litany or the bidding prayer may also be used for the General Intercession. A rubric also allows the Prayer for the Whole State of Christ's Church to be shortened—making of it, in effect, an offertory prayer—when the litany has been said at the beginning of the service or on any weekday that is not a holy day. While this makes sense when the litany has been used, at other times it has the unfortunate effect of eliminating intercessions from the Eucharist altogether.

The Confession likewise clutters the offertory. It is not a part of the historic eucharistic liturgies, and it has never found a stable place in the rite. It makes more sense to use it at the beginning of the service (as in many Reformed rites) or before Communion (as in the 1549 and 1764 rites) or to place it at the end of the Ministry of the Word and before the Peace, with which it has a logical relation (as would be done in 1979), than to leave it as part of the offertory material.

The preliminary offering made at the offertory is highlighted by a rubric explicitly suggesting the two Scottish sentences for this purpose; this provision conforms the American rite more closely to its Scottish origins, but later liturgists would treat this "lesser oblation" as an ambiguous development, and in 1979 we will find no provision for a use of sentences or a hymn at the presentation and no rubric directing the *offering* of the gifts at this point.

Although the rationale makes a point of the "Continuity of the Thanksgiving" (a title of one of its sections), the "Amen" at the end of the Sanctus, which interrupts this continuity, is not removed. Moreover, while the entire eucharistic prayer is given the title "The Consecration," another title, "The Prayer of Consecration" is placed before the post-Sanctus. This prayer itself is given titles in the margins—"The Thanksgiving" for the post-Sanctus, "The Oblation" and "The Invocation" as in previous American books, and "The Supplication" for the last portion of the prayer. By titling the post-Sanctus "The Thanksgiving" the revisers undercut the eucharistic function of the Preface and weakened the eucharistic nature of the whole prayer. The rationale notes the lack of a thanksgiving for creation and for the incarnation, but the text of the rite effectively remedies only the latter. The invocation is explicitly consecratory in a way which now seems to be generally acceptable, as it was not in 1789. The material in "The Supplication" is abbreviated, in response to a general feeling that the eucharistic prayer is unduly long and wordy.

The manual acts are simplified in the rubrics to a "taking" of the bread and the wine during the institution narrative and the fraction is restored to its traditional place after the eucharistic prayer and the Lord's Prayer. The Peace (in a verbal form, with

122

no rubrical direction as to its ceremonial exchange) is placed here also, in its Roman rather than its primitive position. The Benedictus qui venit is restored to the rite, but detached from the Sanctus and placed after the Peace, on somewhat dubious historical precedent. The Agnus Dei is printed in the rite, but as a communion anthem rather than as a fraction anthem (its original function).

In the false euphoria of the superficial growth of mainline churches in the 1950s, Episcopalians on a whole proved little interested in proceeding with this revision. It is perhaps just as well, for it was a "dated" rite when drafted. Bernard Wigan, a leading English liturgist invited to offer a critique, was scathing. Massey Shepherd gives a summary of that critique:[2]

> In particular, he objected to the Commission's working within the framework and structure of the Eucharist, including the form and outline of the Consecration Prayer, as established by Cranmer. For, he said, "Today we know that Cranmer's inherited tradition was a late development and that it could never really be true to Scripture." The Commission was accused of sacrificing "great principles . . . in order to secure a rite which seems likely to be readily acceptable to the majority." Instead, they should have forthrightly submitted a draft—let the criticisms fall where they may—that takes more seriously into account the two principles "that must be the basis of any revision which is to measure up to its evangelical purpose: that our Lord's prayer at the Last Supper was a Jewish thanksgiving-blessing, and that the essential structure of the rite consists of taking, blessing, breaking, giving—in that order."

> The direction of future revision, in fact, was revealed by a new rite of this period which did follow the two principles which Wigan sets forth—the 1950 liturgy of the Church of South India.

Notes to Chapter Four

BIBLIOGRAPHICAL NOTES

Since the 1928 Prayer Book is still in print, it is readily accessible. The 1928 eucharistic rite may be compared to prior American rites with the aid of the critical apparatus printed with this rite in Bernard Wigan, *The Liturgy in English* (London, Oxford University Press, 1961). The rite is also printed in full in Massey Shepherd, *The Oxford American Prayer Book Commentary* (New York, Oxford University Press, 1950), which is the definitive treatment of this edition of the American Prayer Book. The eucharistic liturgy of 1953 is printed in *Prayer Book Studies IV* (New York, Church Pension Fund, 1957).

Massey Shepherd, *The Reform of Liturgical Worship* (New York, Oxford University Press, 1961) and two articles in Malcolm C. Bursin, editor, *Worship Points the Way* (New York, Seabury, 1981)—H. Boone Porter, "Toward an Unofficial History of Episcopal Worship," and Urban T. Holmes, "Education for Liturgy: An Unfinished Symphony in Four Movements"—cover this period in the liturgical history of the Episcopal Church.

The history of the liturgical movement is summarized briefly in Louis Bouyer, *Liturgical Piety* (Notre Dame, 1954) and Lancelot Sheppard, editor, *The People Worship* (New York, Hawthorn Books, 1967).

The bibliography for music given in Chapter 2 also covers this chapter. Significant shifts in architecture were just beginning and affected only a minority of Episcopal parishes. The movement toward use of freestanding altars was beginning, but in the early stages this had little impact on overall architectural design: even A-frame churches were customarily built with their space arranged in Gothic revival patterns.

NOTES ON THE TEXT

1. Urban T. Holmes, "Education for Liturgy: An Unfinished Symphony in Four Movements," in Malcolm C. Bursin, editor, *Worship Points the Way,* page 120.

2. Massey Shepherd, *The Reform of Liturgical Worship,* page 76, referring to Wigan's article, "The Commissioners' Liturgy," *Episcopal Churchnews* CXX, 5 (March 6, 1955).

The Book of Common Prayer 1979

From Prayer Book Studies IV to 1979

Though few realized it at the time, Prayer Books Studies IV represented the end of a line of development in liturgical revision in the American church. All Anglican prayer books up to this point had worked with one or another of Cranmer's rites as their basis. American prayer books had taken as their basic eucharistic rite the 1662 Prayer Book with the 1764 Scottish reconstruction of the eucharistic prayer (somewhat modified). The revisions of 1892 and 1928 and the proposed rite of 1953 introduced changes in the interest of flexibility and enrichment. Now development would follow different lines: Cranmer's work would no longer represent the basis for further development. Even what would eventually become the Rite I Eucharist of 1979, while it retained Cranmer's language, fit the Cranmerian texts into a new structure, and the standard rite of 1979 was Rite II, drafted in contemporary language and so not dependent on Cranmer's texts.

The work that undergirded this shift had been going on for a century. Scholars were recovering a sufficient number of ancient liturgical texts to understand the course of liturgical history in a new way. Ecumenical dialogue was leading toward both theological and liturgical convergence. And the cultural presuppositions which undergirded Prayer Book worship were being eroded: the relationship between church and society was shifting, and the language of the Prayer Book was slowly but inexorably becoming an archaic and somewhat alien tongue.

Dom Gregory Dix probably had a greater impact on liturgical revision than any other single person in the twentieth century. His *Shape of the Liturgy,* inaccurate though it might be in many details and speculative as it might be in some of its reconstructions, changed people's perspective on the liturgy in several ways:

1. It shifted attention from liturgical texts to liturgical structures—as the word "shape" indicates. As a result, scholars began to think of a Eucharist with a Ministry of the Word whose major components were readings with psalmody and the sermon, the prayers, and the peace, and of a Ministry of the Sacrament whose basic structure was fourfold—taking, giving thanks, breaking, and sharing.

2. It taught people to identify strata in liturgical rites—basic components and later additions and developments.

3. It taught people to identify the Jewish roots of Christian worship—an important contribution at a time when comparative religious studies led many to believe that Christian liturgy was heavily dependent on pagan antecedents.

4. It taught people to see the eucharistic prayer as a whole—from the Sursum Corda to the Great Amen.

Dix's great success was as a popularizer; other scholars worked with many of the same insights, but few were so successful at framing them in ways that could be got across to the church at large.

Dix's book has in large measure determined the "shape"—that is, the outline and structure—of every subsequent eucharistic rite, beginning with the liturgy of the Church of South India. In particular, almost every subsequent rite has followed the four-action shape of taking, giving thanks, breaking, and sharing. However, the four actions are not necessarily of equal significance. Recent scholars have treated the taking as a preliminary to giving thanks and the breaking as preliminary to sharing in Communion. They have also pointed out that "taking" is not the same as "offering," so that Dix's offertory theology has come into question.

Dix's work and that of other scholars has also led most churches to recover a full eucharistic prayer—something that the American church never lacked, though most other churches of the Reformation (including the Church of England) did. There is less consensus on the internal structure of that prayer, and a growing conviction that a diversity of structures has existed from the beginning. Dix's insistence that in the Eucharist we consecrate by giving thanks has in fact led to the realization that there is no one formula of words that is essential to effect the consecration of the elements.

Dix's identification of "strata" of materials in liturgical rites has also borne considerable fruit in the development of historical liturgiology, so that scholars today have a better sense of what is basic in a rite and what are secondary materials and developments. Dix's was the first popular presentation of this "structural analysis" of rites. Anton Baumstark's work in comparative liturgics led him to similar conclusions, but he was a scholar's scholar and most of his work was not readily accessible. All of this has resulted in general ecumenical consensus on the basic structure of the eucharistic rite.

Dix's influence has been significant in other areas as well. He was among the first to realize the importance of *The Apostolic Tradition* of Hippolytus, which has had considerable impact (some would say too much impact) on contemporary eucharistic prayers, rites of initiation, and ordination rites. His stress on the eschatological nature of early Christian worship has also affected recent rites.

The Book of Common Prayer 1979 127

Three Roman Catholic scholars had significant influence beyond the boundaries of their own church by the 1950s—Josef Jungmann, Jean Danielou, and Louis Bouyer. Jungmann's scholarship on the Roman Rite became most widely known through his *The Mass of the Roman Rite: Its Origins and Development* (2 vols., New York, Benziger Brothers, 1950) and *The Early Liturgy* (Notre Dame, 1959)—the first a detailed scholarly treatise, the second a more popular presentation. Danielou made accessible to modern readers the patristic vision of the liturgy (particularly the initiatory rites and the Eucharist) in *The Bible and the Liturgy* (Notre Dame, 1956). Perhaps the most successful of the three as a popularizer was Louis Bouyer, whose most influential book was *Liturgical Piety* (Notre Dame, 1954). Drawing on the Swedish Lutheran Yngve Brilioth's *Eucharistic Faith and Practice, Evangelical and Catholic* (translated into English by A. G. Hebert, whom we discussed in the last chapter, and published by the SPCK in London in 1961), he analyzed eucharistic theology under the categories of thanksgiving, sacrifice, memorial, Communion, and mystery. The greatest achievement of this book was to communicate a vision of liturgy as grounded in the Paschal Mystery of Christ's death and resurrection. This theology was inspired by the work of Dom Odo Casel of Maria Laach, but Casel's work was done in German and so largely inaccessible to an English-speaking audience. Bouyer revised it somewhat to take account of the Jewish roots of Christian liturgy and presented it to the English-speaking world. We note that all three of these scholars were published by the press of Notre Dame, whose center for liturgical studies had an important impact on the worship of American churches.

Many found similar inspiration in the work of the Orthodox theologian Alexander Schmemann, whose popular book on liturgical theology, *For the Life of the World* (many editions, currently available from St. Vladimir's Seminary Press, Crestwood, New

York, 1973) was written for a Student Christian Movement Conference. His more scholarly *Introduction to Liturgical Theology* (London, Faith Press, 1966) is less accessible to the average reader but significant as an analysis of liturgical structures.

Comparative anthropology and religion had much to contribute to liturgical thought at this time also. G. van der Leeuw's work, *Religion in Essence and Manifestation* (2 vols., New York, Harper & Row, 1963) was important in introducing this approach, and Mircea Eliade's many works made such insights popular.

In the 1950s and succeeding decades, the Liturgical Movement was reaching its full flower, and the scholars and publications—even the significant ones—are too many to review in a study such as this. Those noted above are those that seem to have had the greatest impact on the course of revision and reform in the Episcopal Church, though each of us would want to add others that were important to us to the list.

The decisive role in preparing the way for liturgical revision and interpreting it to the Episcopal Church was played by seminary faculty. The elder statesman among these faculty was Massey Shepherd, who taught first at the Episcopal Theological School in Cambridge and then at the Church Divinity School of the Pacific. He also directed graduate studies for many years at the summer session at the School of Theology at the University of the South. He had an ecumenical impact through his participation in the Graduate Theological Union in the San Francisco Bay area, and also through his work with the World Council of Churches, the Consultation on Church Union, his observer status at the Second Vatican Council, and his membership in academic societies. His teaching, as well as his *Oxford American Prayer Book Commentary* (New York, Oxford, 1950) created a genuine understanding of the strengths and limitations of the 1928 Book of Common Prayer as the church began to move to the next stage of liturgical revision. He was long an active member of the Standing Liturgical Commission, and was the prime mover behind the alteration of the church's constitution in the 1960s to permit trial use of new rites. It was the final adoption of this amendment in 1967 which set the stage for the whole process of revision. His impact can also be seen on an ecumenical front in the first eucharistic liturgy drafted for the Consultation on Church Union.

H. Boone Porter, who taught liturgics first at Nashotah House and then at the General Seminary, likewise prepared generations of students with an understanding of the liturgy and supervised doctoral studies for a new generation of liturgical scholars in the church. His influence as a teacher was probably greater than that as an author, but his small book, *The Day of Light* (Greenwich, Connecticut, Seabury, 1969), taught many the relationship between the theology of Sunday and the Eucharist and other liturgical rites by which that day was observed.

As the process of revision got underway, the role of Charles Price (Virginia Seminary) as the evangelical spokesman for the emerging rites became increasingly important. Daniel Stevick (Philadelphia Divinity School and Episcopal Divinity School, Cambridge) did significant work on the language of worship and the rites of initiation. Marion Hatchett (School of Theology, University of the South), Leonel Mitchell (Notre Dame and Seabury-Western), Thomas Talley (General Seminary), and Louis Weil (Nashotah House) were also important as interpreters of the revised rites. The important books were Charles Price's final Prayer Book Studies 29 (New York, Church Hymnal Corporation, 1976) which served as the Standing Liturgical Commission's introduction to the Proposed Book of 1976, Daniel Stevick's Supplement to Prayer Book Studies 26 (New York, Church Hymnal Corporation, 1973) on the initiatory rites, and *Liturgy for Living*

(New York, Seabury, 1979), written by Charles Price and Louis Weil for the Church's Teaching Series. Stevick's *Language in Worship: Reflections on a Crisis* (New York, Seabury, 1970) received less attention than it deserved as a major treatment of a sensitive issue.

In interpreting the new Prayer Book, the *Commentary on the American Prayer Book* (New York, Seabury, 1980) by Marion Hatchett enjoys the same status as Massey Shepherd's commentary on the 1928 rite. Other significant works of Hatchett's are *Sanctifying Life, Time, and Space: An Introduction to Liturgical Study* (New York, Seabury, 1976), now a standard text in liturgical history, and *The Making of the First American Book of Common Prayer: 1776–1789* (New York, Seabury, 1982). Leonel Mitchell wrote several popular texts during the period of revision and is author of *Praying Shapes Believing* (Minneapolis, Winston, 1985), a significant theological treatment of the 1979 book. Thomas Talley's major published work is a study of the liturgical year (*The Origins of the Liturgical Year*, New York, Pueblo, 1986).

The ecumenical context of revision is also important. The eucharistic liturgies of the Church of South India and of the Taize Community in France, both ecumenical communities, were early rites in which emerging consensus is revealed. The Episcopal Church was involved in the work of the Faith and Order Division of the World Council of Churches, which produced the document entitled *Baptism, Eucharist, and Ministry: Faith and Order Paper No. 111* (Geneva, World Council of Churches, 1982), setting forth a consensus on both the structure and the theology of the Eucharist. The Church was also involved in the Consultation on Church Union in the United States, which produced similar consensus and an ecumenical rite in the 1960s and a revised eucharistic rite in 1984. Two bilateral dialogues have also been important. After the Second Vatican Council, the Roman Catholic Church, which had embarked on its own course of liturgical revision and reform, entered into international dialogue with the Churches of the Anglican Communion, which produced a consensus statement on the Eucharist (The Windsor Statement, 1971) and an elucidation (The Salisbury Statement, 1979). These were part of the Final Report (printed in 1982 and issued by Forward Movement in Cincinnati), but progress has stalled since that time. A bilateral dialogue with the Lutheran churches in the United States resulted in a covenant between three Lutheran churches and the Episcopal Church in the 1980s which allows for joint celebration of the sacrament. These three churches produced in their own *Lutheran Book of Worship* (Minneapolis, Augsburg, 1978) a eucharistic rite which closely resembles that of the Book of Common Prayer.

This ecumenical convergence meant that the natural allies of both Evangelicals and Catholics in the Episcopal Church were producing very similar rites as the Prayer Book was being revised, and this did much to undercut partisan strife in the process of revision.

The Process of Revision: 1967–1979

By the 1950s, the Standing Liturical Commission was convinced that the constitutional provisions for revision of the Prayer Book were inadequate. The legislative process was cumbersome, with a greatly increased number of bishops and lay and clerical delegates, and an always crowded agenda. Perhaps the principal problem with the process is revealed, however, in the 1928 office for the Visitation of the Sick. The theology of that rite is a vast improvement over what was found in previous Prayer Books. But in a pastoral context, the service simply proved unusable in its printed form. The problem with the legislative process of revision, above all else, is that it provides no way to test out revisions in actual use before they are adopted.

The Commission was convinced that it was imperative to make constitutional provision for trial use of proposed revisions, and urged this action on the Conventions of 1952, 1955, and 1958 without success. To make its case, the Commission published, as Prayer Book Studies XV, a paper setting out the rationale for trial use. Massey Shepherd, though not a delegate to that convention, was granted the opportunity to speak to the issue there. The amendment proposed was not adopted that year, but such an amendment did pass its first reading in 1964, and passage of a second reading in 1967 made it possible for the church to undertake revision in a new way. Associated Parishes had by this time committed itself to revision and, through its conferences, newsletter *(Open),* and tracts, was an effective advocate of the revised rites which were to come.

The Standing Liturgical Commission was prepared to take advantage of this constitutional change. In 1966 it published a proposed eucharistic liturgy, *The Liturgy of the Lord's Supper,* as Prayer Book Studies XVII. A new era in the church's worship had begun. *The Liturgy of the Lord's Supper* did what the rite of Prayer Book Studies IV had not done: it based its work on the current fruits of liturgical scholarship. The rite followed the "shape" which Dom Gregory Dix had identified, rearranging the components of the liturgy by removing from the offertory the General Intercession and the Confession and by restoring the Gloria in excelsis to its traditional position at the beginning of the Ministry of the Word. The rite was written in what might be called modified traditional English: like the Revised Standard Version of the Bible and some of the materials added to the Prayer Book in 1928, it continued to address God in the second person singular as "thou," but addressed people in the familiar second person plural as "you."

The rite was authorized for trial use in 1967, and a procedure was adopted for surveying the church's reaction to the rite through a questionnaire to be returned by those who had used it. The response of the church revealed several things:

1. Extensive liturgical education would be necessary for the whole church if liturgical revision was to find acceptance and to result in genuine liturgical renewal.

2. The new "shape" or outline of the rite met with a generally positive response.

3. The language of the rite pleased almost no one. Some preferred the retention of traditional language for both God and people; others preferred to move to a genuinely contemporary diction for worship and to address both God and people as "you."

4. People's response to the rite was often symptomatic of their response to the cultural convulsions of the time as their impact was being felt in the life of the church.

The Commission took seriously what the church was saying about language, and as a result adopted the policy of providing forms of the regular services of the church (Morning and Evening Prayer and the Eucharist) and the Burial Office in traditional Cranmerian language (called at first "First Service" and later "Rite I"), while making contemporary language (called "Second Service" or "Rite II" for those services which had traditional forms) the normative language of the book.

It was on the third and fourth issues that the often acrimonious debate about the revision of the Prayer Book focused. Traditionalists in the "Society for the Preservation of the Book of Common Prayer" and similar groups fiercely upheld the language of the 1928 Book, but underlying the passion of their position was their response to the cultural convulsions of American society in the

1960s and 1970s. This was the era of the Civil Rights Movement, the Peace Movement, the Women's Movement, and the Youth Movement. Society seemed to be becoming unglued. All of these movements had their impact on the life of the church and, directly or indirectly, on the church's worship. The controversies weakened the authority of leadership in both church and society, and raised questions about the relationship of church and state, on the one hand, and the sacred and the secular on the other.

But language was the place where the issue surfaced most insistently. Opposition to liturgical revision seems to have been concentrated among conservative Anglo-Catholic clergy and latitudinarian low-church laity. Clergy often raised theological objections, although most scholars concluded that the revisions were in fact truer to Catholic tradition than the 1928 Book and opponents often simply revealed their lack of knowledge of the theological or liturgical tradition in any depth. Lay opposition focused on the loss of the cultural heritage of Cranmerian language and also on uneasiness about the breakdown of the alliance of church and state and traditional moral consensus. The very different concerns of clerical and lay opposition made for an unstable coalition, and those who left the Episcopal Church continued to fragment in their new groupings.

In the debate over language, the use of "thou" for God was universally perceived as conveying a sense of reverential awe and distance. Only the more perceptive realized that this was a complete reversal of its original meaning. In sixteenth-century usage, the second person singular ("thou") was used for familiars, lovers, children, and social inferiors. The second person plural ("you") was used for social equals and superiors as a polite form. That means that when it was adopted, "thou" was an intimate form of address to God: exactly the opposite of the current perception of its meaning.

By 1970 the Standing Liturgical Commission had drafted a complete revision of the Book of Common Prayer, issued in a series of Prayer Book Studies which carefully elaborated the rationale for changes. These services were then collected in *Services for Trial Use* (the "Green Book") authorized by the General Convention in that year. The results of trial use of this book resulted in the revisions published in 1973 in *Authorized Services,* popularly known from its cover as the "Zebra Book." By 1976 the Commission was ready to present a "Draft Proposed Book of Common Prayer" which, with minor adjustments, passed its first reading that year and was adopted as the Book of Common Prayer on its second reading in 1979.

Through the entire process the Rev. Leo Malania, working as part-time coordinator, and Howard Galley, working as editorial assistant, kept work on track—Fr. Malania through his tact, pastoral sensitivity, and patience; Mr. Galley not only through his editorial skills but also through his encyclopedic knowledge of historic liturgies. To these men the church owes an enormous debt of gratitude.

To assist with the process of revision and trial use, the Standing Liturgical Commission called for the creation in each diocese of a liturgical commission. The chairs of these commissions were gathered to pool their resources, to receive training, and to plan strategy in a conference organized with the help of the Associated Parishes in 1971 and have continued to meet annually since that time. They eventually organized as the Association of Diocesan Liturgy and Music Commissions. This Association, along with the diocesan commissions, has provided a means of communication and liaison between the national church and the local church and has had significant impact on the adoption and implementation of the Book of Common Prayer 1979.

The process was controversial and the debate at times heated. The danger of polarization was very real. But Episcopalians began for the first time to learn to think liturgically, rather than to rely on their clergy to do their liturgical thinking for them. The church also owes a great debt to its parish clergy, for they not only had to catch up and keep abreast liturgically, they also had to oversee the process of education and change in their parishes and to deal with the considerable conflict that trial use and the adoption of a new prayer book engendered.

The 1979 Rite and Its Rationale

We turn now to an outline of the 1979 rite, "The Holy Eucharist: The Liturgy for the Proclamation of the Word of God and the Celebration of the Holy Communion." It is printed in three forms—Rite I (traditional language), Rite II (contemporary language), and An Order for Celebrating the Holy Eucharist. In our outline we use the titles for the two major parts given in the subtitle to the rite as a whole—The Proclamation of the Word of God (shortened in the body of the text to "The Word of God" and also referred to elsewhere in the book as "The Liturgy of the Word" or "The Ministry of the Word") and the Celebration of the Holy Communion (shortened in the body of the text to "The Holy Communion"). For subsections and individual components, we use titles given in the text, along with the descriptions given in "An Order for Celebrating the Holy Eucharist." Variants between the two rites are noted. Components which are optional are marked with an asterisk before them.

The Proclamation of the Word of God

"The People and Priest Gather in the Lord's Name"

RITE I
*Hymn, psalm, or anthem

*Acclamation
Collect for Purity
*Summary of the Law or *Decalogue
Kyrie (threefold, sixfold, or ninefold, Greek or English)
or Trisagion
and/or Gloria in excelsis or song of praise (when appointed)

RITE II
*Hymn, Psalm, or Anthem
Acclamation
*Collect for Purity
Gloria in excelsis or song of praise (when appointed)
or Kyrie (threefold, sixfold, or ninefold, Greek or English)
or Trisagion

"They Proclaim and Respond to the Word of God"
The Word of God
Salutation and collect
First Lesson
*Psalm, hymn, or anthem
    Gradual psalm appointed in lectionary
*Second Lesson
*Psalm, hymn, or anthem
Gospel with responses before and after
The Sermon
The Nicene Creed (on Sundays and other Major Feasts)
    ICET or 1928 (Rite I)
    ICET (Rite II)

"They Pray for the World and the Church"
The Prayers of the People

RITE I

Prayer for the Whole State of Christ's Church and the
World
or in any of the six forms given
or according to an outline of topics

RITE II

In any of the six forms given
or according to an outline of topics

"They Exchange the Peace"

The Confession (may be omitted on occasion)

RITE I

Invitation, Confession (2 forms), Absolution,
*Comfortable Words

RITE II

*Sentence, Invitation, Confession, Absolution

The Peace

The Celebration of the Holy Communion

"They Prepare the Table"

*Sentence or bidding
*Hymn, psalm, or anthem
Collection of alms
Presentation and Placement of bread, wine, and money or
other gifts

"They Make Eucharist" (Give Thanks)
The Great Thanksgiving

> RITE I (Eucharistic Prayers I and II)
> Salutation and Sursum Corda
> Preface
> Sanctus/*Benedictus
> Continuation
> Great Amen
> Lord's Prayer

> RITE II (Eucharistic Prayers A, B, C, D)
> Salutation and Sursum Corda
> Preface
> Sanctus/Benedictus
> Continuation with Memorial Acclamation
> Great Amen
> Lord's Prayer (Traditional or Contemporary/ICET)

The Breaking of the Bread

"They Break the Bread"

> Fraction
> *Pascha Nostrum and/or *Agnus Dei or other anthem
> *Prayer of Humble Access (Rite I only)

"They Share the Gifts of God"

> Invitation (optional, Rite I)
> Communion (various words of administration)
> *Hymns, psalms, anthems
> Postcommunion prayer (2 alternatives in Rite II)
> *Hymn
> Blessing (optional, Rite II)
> Dismissal (four forms; optional, Rite I)

CHAPTER FIVE:

Alternative Entrance Rites

1. *The Great Litany, ending with the Kyrie*
(service continues at the Kyrie in the Eucharist)
2. *The Order of Worship for the Evening, ending with the Phos hilaron*
(service continues with the salutation and collect)
3. *A Penitential Order*
(service continues with Kyrie, Trisagion, or Gloria)
(confession omitted before the Peace)

Morning or Evening Prayer as the Proclamation of the Word

*Sentence
*Invitation, Confession, Absolution

Preces
Invitatory Psalm or Canticle or Phos hilaron or hymn (evening)
Psalm(s)

Lesson
Canticle
Lesson   or Gospel
Canticle
Gospel   (read earlier if only two lessons are used)

Sermon
Apostles or Nicene Creed
Salutation and Collect
Prayers of the People

The Shape: The impact of Dom Gregory Dix's "shape" on the 1979 rites is immediately apparent. By restoring the Gloria to its original position in the entrance rite, by placing the "offertory" *after* (rather than before) the Prayers of the People and the Confession, and by moving the fraction from the manual acts during the Institution Narrative, the revisers have restored the primitive structure. The sermon now follows immediately after the Gospel. The Peace has been restored, with preference given to its primitive position before the offertory rather than its 1549 and Roman position (which is, however, rubrically permissible) before Communion.

The Decalogue with its responses and its collect, which interrupted the flow of the service, has been removed from the body of the text, although it may still be used with Rite I if desired.

Other material, which accumulated in what Robert Taft calls the "soft spots" in the rite (the entrance, the offertory, and the communion and postcommunion)[1] has also been removed or made optional. At the entrance, the Summary of the Law has been made optional in Rite I and removed from Rite II; in Rite II, the Collect for Purity is optional. The primitive shape of the entrance consisted of a greeting; to this an entrance song and collect were early additions. In Rite II, something of this early shape can be restored by using the acclamation, followed by a canticle or hymn for the entrance song and by the salutation and collect. Ideally, no entrance song or canticle would be required at services without music; the Canadian *Book of Alternative Services* (Toronto, Anglican Book Centre, 1985), which contains the Canadian contemporary language rites, has in fact adopted this pattern.

At the offertory, the provision for a presentation hymn has been removed, along with the direction that the celebrant "offer" the bread and wine; the temptation to add offertory prayers was also resisted. In the Scottish-American tradition (unlike the earlier Cranmerian tradition), the gifts are offered in the text of the Great Thanksgiving; that makes a preliminary offering, or "lesser oblation" when the table is prepared, redundant. The offertory in the text of the rite is uncluttered; the temptation, however, to add gestures or prayers not found in the text is not always resisted in practice.

The removal of the Gloria in excelsis and of rubrical permission to add collects before the Blessing has left the rite relatively uncluttered at the fraction and Communion. Hymns are permitted here and serve as "cover music"; the one bit of clutter which remains is the not infrequent practice of using both the Pascha nostrum ("Christ our Passover") and the Agnus Dei ("O Lamb of God"); both are fraction anthems, and one or the other should be chosen.

The Order for Celebrating the Holy Eucharist provides an outline for the celebration (quoted in our outline above): the outline sets out the necessary components and allows the use of any eucharistic prayer in the book, or the drafting of a prayer appropriate to the occasion on the basis of two partial forms that are given. This rite is not intended, however, for use at the principal Sunday or weekly Eucharist. The structural concerns of the revisers are especially clear in this order.

Flexibility: the Entrance Rite: Flexibility is seen in the provision of alternative entrance rites—the Penitential Order (which, unlike the 1953 rite, includes the Confession); the Great Litany (with its Kyrie becoming that of the Eucharist, as in 1953, and rubrics providing that the Prayers of the People in their normal place may then be omitted); or the Order of Worship for the Evening (which makes the entrance a "lamplighting" rite for an evening service).

Flexibility: The Use of Morning or Evening Prayer: The provision for use of Morning or Evening Prayer makes these an alternative Ministry of the Word, rather than a supplement to the eucharistic Ministry of the Word. Rubrics provide for a smooth integration of the two rites. It might have been preferable, however, to follow the Apostles' Creed with the Prayers of the People and to conclude these prayers with the Collect of the Day, rather than to place it between the Creed and the Prayers of the People.

Flexibility: Baptism: When there are baptisms, the Eucharist is now given an abbreviated entrance rite and the baptismal liturgy itself is integrated into the Eucharist, being incorporated between the Sermon and the Peace. This reintegrates what was becoming a private rite into the public worship of the church.

A Comprehensive Service of Word and Sacrament: All of these provisions finally achieve what every American Prayer Book since 1789 has aimed at—a comprehensive service of word and sacrament. They achieve this in a single rite—not by combining parts of three or even four rites (Morning Prayer, Baptism, the Litany, and the Eucharist). The Eucharist appears to be becoming, in parochial practice as well as in theory, "the principal act of Christian worship on the Lord's Day and other Major Feasts." A similar recovery seems to be underway in many other denominations as well.

The three-year lectionary for the principal service (whether the Eucharist or Morning Prayer) provides for a systematic reading of most of the New Testament and a substantial proportion of the Old as well. The lectionary is an ecumenical venture, based (as are the lectionaries of most other American denominations) on that adopted by the Roman Catholic Church after the Second Vatican Council. It provides for Sundays and Major Feasts an Old Testament Reading, a psalm, an Epistle, and a Gospel. The reading of the Old Testament and the psalms is thus restored to the Eucharist. Up until this time, the Episcopal Church had done its systematic reading of the Bible at the Daily Office; but a majority of its members have never participated in the office daily. The reorganization of the eucharistic lectionary is thus a significant gain in the effort to achieve biblical literacy for the church.

While Morning or Evening Prayer may be used in place of the eucharistic Ministry of the Word, this seems in practice to work better on weekdays (when the office lectionary is used) than on Sundays and feasts. On Sundays, many elements of the office may be incorporated into the eucharistic Ministry of the Word, however, in the following ways:

Venite, Jubilate	psalm at the entrance
Easter Canticle	opening canticle (in place of Gloria) or fraction anthem
Old Testament lesson	first lesson at the Eucharist
Psalm	gradual psalm at the Eucharist
Office Canticles	"Song of praise" in place of Gloria or response to the second lesson
Apostles' Creed	Renewal of baptismal vows on baptismal feasts
Office Collects	Collect at the Intercession

In this way much of the heritage of the Anglican office can be preserved at the Sunday Eucharist.

As we have seen, the baptismal rite can also be integrated into the eucharistic rite for Sundays and feasts without unduly lengthening it; these are the normative times for baptism.

The intercessions of the eucharistic rites are also comprehensive. The rubrics set out the topics of intercession normally to be followed:

The Universal Church, its members and its mission
The Nation and all in authority
The welfare of the world

The concerns of the local community
Those who suffer and those in any trouble
The departed (with commemoration of a saint when appropriate)

The Prayer for the Whole State of Christ's Church and the World (printed in the text of Rite I), the six forms for use as the Prayers of the People with either Rite I or Rite II, and the Great Litany (which may be used at the entrance in place of the Prayers of the People) all follow this outline of topics, and other forms of intercession which follow the outline may also be used. Particular concerns may be incorporated in various ways in all these forms.

The range of doctrinal themes incorporated into the eucharistic rite has also been expanded—primarily in the new eucharistic prayers, which all include a thanksgiving for creation and the incarnation as well as for the atonement, and reflect a heightened eschatological awareness. In ordinary time (after Epiphany and Pentecost) the three prefaces for the Lord's Day highlight the doctrines of creation, the resurrection, and the Spirit, which are all related to the theology of the Lord's Day.

Eucharistic Prayers: Dix's influence can also be seen in the structure of the eucharistic prayers. As the title given to these prayers in the text of the rite, "The Great Thanksgiving," indicates, they emphasize the theme of thanksgiving. The unity of the prayers, from the salutation and Sursum Corda to the final "Amen," stands outs. The removal of the "Amen" in the Sanctus, the decision to print the proper prefaces outside the body of the rites, and the deletion of titles before the post-Sanctus ("The Prayer of Consecration") and elsewhere in the course of the prayer ("The Oblation" and "The Invocation") emphasize the treatment of the prayers as an integrated whole. We consecrate by giving thanks, as Dix taught, and the 1979 rite operates with this assumption.

Eucharistic Prayer I preserves the 1928 text intact (except for the removal of the "Amen" on the Sanctus and the optional provision for the addition of the Benedictus qui venit), and the other eucharistic prayers (except Prayer C and Form I) follow the traditional structure of the Scottish-American prayers:

Sursum Corda, Preface, Sanctus (thanksgiving)
Post-Sanctus (thanksgiving continued)
Institution Narrative
Anamnesis/Oblation
Invocation of the Spirit
Supplication
Doxology and Great Amen

In Eucharistic Prayer C and Form II, the invocation precedes the Institution Narrative (along Alexandrian and Roman lines).

Eucharistic Prayer II is a reworked version of Prayer I, along the lines proposed in the 1953 rite. Prayer A is a contemporary composition, thematically close to the traditional Scottish-American prayers. Prayer B is a modern composition which is influenced by Hippolytus. Prayer C is intentionally contemporary in its themes and incorporates frequent responses. Prayer D is an ecumenical version of the Alexandrian form of the anaphora (eucharistic prayer) of St. Basil. Forms I and II of the Order for Celebrating the Holy Eucharist are partial forms which serve as a basis for drafting eucharistic prayers appropriate to the occasion. The new eucharistic prayers of the rite use a much broader range of language to describe the saving work of Christ, utilizing the many images found in the Bible itself to draw out the meaning of this work.[2]

The Eucharistic Theology of the Prayers: In the new Eucharistic Prayers the American church has moved toward a clear affirmation of the real presence (without closely defining it). The invocation in each of the new prayers is explicitly consecratory; the 1928 invocation (retained in Eucharistic Prayer I) easily lends itself to a receptionist interpretation. The Rite I postcommunion prayer has also been slightly recast to avoid receptionist phrases.

The doctrine of consecration which underlies these prayers is twofold. First, as we have noted, the drafters worked with the conviction that we consecrate by giving thanks according to Christ's institution and they sought to avoid the idea of consecration by a verbal formula—whether that formula be the "words of institution" or "the invocation." Nevertheless, they also worked with the Anglican preference for an invocation of the Spirit as the best way of giving expression to the function of the prayer in setting apart the bread and wine as means of Christ's sacramental presence.

The doctrine of eucharistic sacrifice is articulated in several ways:

1. the sacrifice of praise and thanksgiving (which finds verbal expression in various ways);

2. the Eucharist as the anamnesis of Christ's sacrifice (usually found in the section of the eucharistic prayer immediately after the Institution Narrative);

3. the self-oblation of the worshipers;

4. the oblation of the bread and wine as means both of the anamnesis of Christ's sacrifice and of our self-oblation (which finds expression in the offertory bidding, which speaks of the oblations of our life and labor and in the explicit verbal oblation usually found in the text of the eucharistic prayers).

The catechism gives a carefully worded exposition of the eucharistic sacrifice:

CHAPTER FIVE:

. . .the Eucharist, as the church's sacrifice of praise and thanksgiving, is the way by which the sacrifice of Christ is made present, and in which he unites us to his one offering of himself.

The gifts of bread and wine are to be presented by representatives of the congregation, but they are not offered when presented (as they were in the 1928 rite), but in the course of the Great Thanksgiving. This carefully nuanced doctrine would have been made clearer if the "taking" had not been called the "offertory" in the rubrics; however, the revisers did avoid using "Offertory" as a subtitle in the text of the rite.

Charles Price in Prayer Book Studies 29 sums up the theology of the eucharistic prayers very skillfully:[3]

The force of the Offering . . . , following the Absolution and Peace, is that a community of baptized persons, accepted and forgiven by God, bring the gifts they are commanded to offer, and offer themselves through these gifts, to be transformed and renewed by the Body and Blood of Christ, his very life, made accessible to them through bread and wine according to his promise. The elements are the "means effectual" of communion and grace.

The Eucharist as the Context for Other Rites: The 1979 Book makes the Eucharist the normal context for various pastoral offices—Confirmation, Commitment to Christian Service, Marriage, the Ministry to the Sick, and the Burial Office—as well as such services as Ordination, the Celebration of a New Ministry, and the Consecration of a Church. In prior Prayer Books, services such as these, when celebrated with the Eucharist, were *added on* to it; now they are closely integrated into its structure. Their distinctive elements are generally inserted in one or more of the following places:

1. The Entrance Rite;

2. After the Gospel (with Sermon and Creed, when appointed) and before the Peace;

3. In the postcommunion.

In many cases, a proper collect and proper lessons are also provided for the Ministry of the Word. Proper liturgies for special days also incorporate appropriate elements in one or more of these places.

The Participatory Character of the Rites: A strongly marked feature of the 1979 Eucharist is its highly participatory character. All the new formulas for the Prayers of the People call for either verbal responses by the congregation or (Form II) silent intercession in the course of the petitions. A response may be used with the form printed in the text of Rite I as well. All the Eucharistic Prayers of Rite II have a memorial acclamation (in Eucharistic Prayer A, "Christ has died, . . .") and Prayer C is responsive throughout. Responsive forms are also given for the opening acclamation, the alternative conclusion of the lessons, and the dismissal. The baptismal rite has a greatly increased part for the congregation, particularly in the renewal of the baptismal covenant by the congregation. In the case of the Prayer of Humble Access (Rite I) and the postcommunion prayers, the congregation may now join in prayers once assigned to the celebrant.

Roles for particular lay persons are also explicitly set out: they normally read the lessons before the Gospel, they may lead the intercessions, and as representatives of the congregation they present the bread and wine.

The characteristic and distinctive roles of the three orders of ordained ministers are clearly specified in a similar fashion. A bishop or presbyter normally presides at the Proclamation of the

Word of God and must preside at the Celebration of the Holy Communion. Other (bishops and) presbyters stand at the table with the celebrant and join in the consecration of the gifts, in breaking the bread, and in distributing Communion. A deacon reads the Gospel, may lead the prayers of the people, prepares the table, clears the table, and gives the dismissal.

An important related development has been the reintegration of children into the parish Eucharist. In the early stages of revision, the decision was made to admit children to Communion before Confirmation. The Book of Common Prayer itself now sets no requirements for admission to Communion other than Baptism, and in some parishes it is customary for even infants to receive. This reintegration of children into the parish Eucharist is still in process: to be successful, it requires a style of worship which engages all ages, and we are still working to develop such a style. In the meantime, it is not uncommon in places where children are not yet present throughout the Eucharist for them to go to classes during the Ministry of the Word and to join in the parish Eucharist at the Peace. While this is not an ideal solution, it is a significant advance from a time when children were all but banished from parish worship.

The Architectural, Ceremonial, and Musical Setting of the 1979 Rite

The only explicit architectural requirements of the 1979 rite are the recommendation that lessons be read from a lectern (with the suggestion that the Gospel may also be read from the lectern and the Sermon preached there—thus making a separate pulpit unnecessary) and the removal of any requirement that Communion be received kneeling (thus making an altar rail unnecessary). It is rubrically possible to use most churches in the same way for the 1979 rite as they were used for the 1928 rite.

However, the ideal setting for the celebration of the Eucharist according to the 1979 rite does differ from the design of churches which has become customary. The "one-room" spaces which were common before the Gothic Revival are, in fact, much better suited to celebrations according to the 1979 Book than the "two-room" spaces which became all but universal in the course of the nineteenth century. Marion Hatchett discusses the architectural implications of the 1979 rite in Occasional Paper 6, issued by the Standing Liturgical Commission.

The architectural implications of the 1979 rite would call for the following elements in architectural design:

1. A suitable lectern should be provided for the readings at the Proclamation of the Word of God in the Eucharist. This should be easily visible and so placed that readers may be heard without difficulty. It may also serve as a Gospel lectern and a place for preaching, rendering a separate pulpit unnecessary.

2. Clergy seating should be provided in a place where the clergy may easily be seen and heard when presiding at the Proclamation of the Word of God. The rubrics no longer require that the clergy stand before the altar to preside at this part of the Eucharist, and seating behind the altar or in another suitable location should be planned.

3. A freestanding table should be provided for the Celebration of the Holy Communion. It should, so far as possible, be in the midst of the people rather than separated from them. Ideally, people should be gathered around three sides. An altar rail is not necessary. If a parish prefers to continue administering Communion to people kneeling, movable kneeling benches on the level of congregational seating are more accessible than an altar rail and create less of a sense of separation.

4. Choir seating should be provided in a place that does not position the choir between the altar and the congregation and that enables them to support congregational singing. Acoustical considerations are important in placement of both the choir and the musical instrument used to accompany singing. The instrument should be located near the choir and should speak directly into the area for congregational seating. Depending on circumstances, choir members may be behind the altar, or to the side, front, or back of the congregational seating. Galleries have the unfortunate effect of cutting choir members off from the action of the liturgy.

5. Congregational seating should be placed around three sides of the altar when possible. Movable seating allows greater flexibility in the use of space than fixed pews.

6. The font should be located so that Baptism may be administered in the sight of the congregation. A font at the rear or the front of the church usually works best for this purpose. It should hold a substantial amount of water and should be large enough to allow an infant to be baptized by immersion. Our baptismal practice is in a period of transition at present. In the future we may find it desirable to provide a baptismal pool for adult baptisms; in this case it will be important to consider nearby dressing facilities as well for adults baptized by partial or full immersion.

Lectern, table, clergy seating, and font are the visual foci of the Sunday Eucharist. They should be configured in whatever way works best in a given situation. At times they may all be placed on a chancel platform; this platform, however, works best if it resembles a thrust stage (with the audience seated around it on three sides) rather than a stage behind a proscenium arch (the plan of traditional theaters). In such a situation the platform is better located in the center of the long side of the church, rather than at one of the narrower ends of the building. Such a plan will be found in the last of the figures in the schematic architectural plans in the Appendix. Another possible arrangement places the congregational seating along the sides as in collegiate chapels, and locates font, clergy seating, lectern, and table along a wide center aisle. Adequate processional space should be provided for rites such as the Liturgy of the Palms and the Great Vigil of Easter. Accessibility to the handicapped should always be a consideration. The space for worship should also be adaptable to the requirements of marriages and burials.

Thoughtful Episcopalians of all schools of churchmanship have realized the need to rethink the ceremonial style in which the Eucharist is celebrated, and this has effectively undercut the partisan nature of various ceremonial usages. All schools have come, on the whole, to prefer a simpler and more functional style of ceremonial action and gesture, and to avoid the often arcane and allegorical interpretation that was borrowed from medieval usages in the nineteenth century. Since a similar trend is evident in other denominations as well, there is a considerable measure of ecumenical convergence on this matter. The rubrics of the Prayer Book are flexible and allow for appropriate adaptation to particular situations. The "noble simplicity" for which the *Constitution on the Sacred Liturgy* of the Second Vatican Council called expresses the predominant outlook of most today. Contemporary liturgists favor a ceremonial style which emphasizes the basic structure of the rite, brings out its meaning, and avoids obscuring this with secondary elements. At the same time, there is a new freedom to use dramatic ceremony when appropriate—as in the rites of Holy Week and the Great Vigil of Easter.

One notable difference in the 1979 rite is the preference expressed in the rubrics for standing instead of kneeling as the posture for prayer. This is a recovery of earlier Christian tradition in place of the predominant usage of the Middle Ages.

The current trend is for all those who vest for worship to wear the alb as their basic vestment, and for the celebrant and assistants to use eucharistic vestments of simple cut and ornamentation. Candles, color, art, and even incense—if used with restraint—are more widely perceived as appropriate in Christian worship.

This ceremonial style is gradually gaining ground in the Episcopal Church. The "overlay" of the older Roman Catholic ceremonial style on the Prayer Book rite is deeply ingrained by now, however, and has by no means disappeared, incongruous though it often is.

The use of music has also undergone a shift. *The Hymnal 1982, The Gradual Psalms, The Altar Book, The Anglican Chant Psalter, Music for Ministers and Congregations,* and other nonofficial books provide for a full choral celebration when desired. *The Hymnal 1982* was specifically designed to meet the requirements of the 1979 Book. The decision about what is to be sung and what is to be said, however, is less closely correlated than formerly to issues of churchmanship. Other criteria are followed in determining what use of music is appropriate in a particular situation. Music properly understood is a heightened form of human speech and so understood is an integral part of public worship, not an optional ornamentation. As Benedict reminds us, "One who sings prays twice."

A greater variety of musical styles and of musical instruments is now common. Folk and popular music became enormously popular at an early stage in revision. While such music is still common, on the whole the church is more discriminating in its use than it was at first. Gradual psalmody (in a variety of styles) has become common, but the traditional psalmody at the introit, offertory, and communion is less frequently used by Episcopalians (and by Roman Catholics) than it once was.

The Book of Common Prayer 1979   155

With a greater use of responsorial music, the cantor has gained new prominence—in a way recovering part of the role of the old parish clerk. At present, care is also usually taken that the choir does not usurp parts of the liturgy that properly belong to the congregation.

Notes to Chapter Five

BIBLIOGRAPHIC NOTES

The Church Pension Fund and its affiliate, the Church Hymnal Corporation, are the official publishers of liturgical and musical texts for the Episcopal Church. They have been the publishers for all the Prayer Book Studies; only the final study in the series, 29R (the introduction to the 1979 Book) and the final study on the initiatory rites, the supplement to 26 (in a revised edition) are generally in print at this time. The eucharistic liturgy of PBS IV and *The Liturgy of the Lord's Supper* (1967), *Services for Trial Use* (1970), *Authorized Services* (1973), *The Draft Proposed Book of Common Prayer* (1975), *The Proposed Book of Common Prayer* (1976), and *The Book of Common Prayer* (1979) were all published by them. Only the 1979 book is now in print. They are publishers as well for the official liturgical and musical texts which are adjuncts to the rite—*The Altar Book, The Book of Occasional Services, Lectionary Texts, The Hymnal 1982, Gradual Psalms, Music for Ministers and Congregations,* and a series of Hymnal Studies. In 1987 they issued the Occasional Papers of the Standing Liturgical Commission in a single volume.

Bibliographical data on important works which had an impact on the 1979 Book, on liturgical texts of other churches and on ecumenical rites and studies are given in the text of the chapter.

The history of the 1979 Book is briefly chronicled in two articles in *Worship Points the Way,* edited by Malcom C. Burson (New York, Seabury, 1981)—H. Boone Porter's "Toward an Unofficial History of Episcopal Worship," and Urban T. Holmes's "Education for Liturgy: An Unfinished Symphony in Four

Movements." Urban Holmes underestimates the importance of Dom Gregory Dix in the liturgical revisions of this century, in the author's opinion; Paul V. Marshall's appended notes to the 1983 Seabury Press edition of Dix's *Shape of the Liturgy* and Kenneth Stevenson, *Gregory Dix—Twenty Five Years On* (Bramcote Notts, Grove Books, 1977) serve as a corrective in this regard. Kenneth Stevenson sets the American revision in a larger perspective in *Eucharist and Offering* (New York, Pueblo, 1986).

NOTES ON THE TEXT

1. Robert Taft, SJ, *Beyond East and West: Problems in Liturgical Understanding* (Washington, Pastoral Press, 1984), chapters 10 and 11. These two chapters survey the development of the structural analysis of liturgical texts, with particular reference to the Eucharist. The main scholars in this century who have been involved with this school of interpretation are Anton Baumstark, H. Engberding, Juan Mateos, and Taft himself. Dix's *Shape* follows a similar method and his work influenced many of the scholars cited above, but he cannot really be counted as a member of this school.

2. Cf. Charles Price, *Prayer Book Studies 29* Revised, (New York, Church Hymnal Corporation, pp. 38–40.

3. Ibid., p. 78.

The Present
and the Future

1. A Liturgical Watershed:
A Review of How We Got Where We Are Today

The forms of our worship do not change through a course of slow, steady evolution, but rather undergo significant development at critical moments in the church's history. The Reformation was one such moment. The Prayer Books of 1549 and 1552 represent a revolution in the worship of English-speaking Christians. The Prayer Books of 1559, 1611, and 1662 represent a consolidation of the achievements of 1549 and 1552. In the first part of Chapter 1 we reviewed the development of the English rite.

Another course of development in Anglican worship can be traced in the development of the Scottish Eucharist, reviewed in the last part of Chapter 1. After an ill-fated beginning in 1637, the course of this development was interrupted for the rest of the century, but again got underway shortly after 1700 and reached its term in the Scottish Communion Office of 1764.

The American Eucharist is heir of both of these traditions. Working with the English rite as its basis, it adopted within this rite the Scottish eucharistic prayer in a modified form. Chapter 2 reviews the story of how this happened.

Another liturgical revolution, however, interrupted the development of the American rite. The Oxford Movement in the mid-nineteenth century and the Gothic revival which soon followed it overlaid much that was alien in the Scottish-American eucharistic tradition. These developments affected not so much the text of the Eucharist as the way it was understood, celebrated, and experienced. Chapters 3 and 4 trace this part of the story.

The Liturgical Movement of the twentieth century represents perhaps as great a liturgical revolution as the Reformation of the sixteenth century. In some respects it achieved, for the first time, some of the goals set in the Reformation. As we have seen, the 1549 and the 1552 Prayer Books understood the Eucharist as "the principal act of Christian worship" on Sundays and other major feasts and attempted (unsuccessfully) to secure its celebration on these days. This was a goal of both the Scottish and the early American rites as well—as can be seen in the Scottish catechism which Bishop Seabury published for use in his diocese. The Oxford Movement also sought to achieve this goal and did succeed in establishing an early Sunday celebration in almost every parish, but in so doing compromised its goal of making the Eucharist the *principal* Sunday service, and also (by its advocacy of a daily celebration) obscured the relation between the theology of Sunday and the theology of the Eucharist and undercut the rationale of the Daily Office. For 400 years Anglicans were unable to realize this goal. With the 1979 rite the goal seems to be within reach, as more and more parishes make the Eucharist their chief Sunday service—a comprehensive service of Word and Sacrament.

The sixteenth-century reformers sought to return to the worship of the primitive church, but lacked the historical materials to make an accurate assessment of the true shape of this worship. In terms of the Eucharist, we see this most clearly in the eucharistic prayer and the general intercession or Prayers of the People.

Cranmer's eucharistic prayer of 1549 was an inspired guess; his prayer of 1552 was less happy. The Scottish reconstruction of the prayer in 1764, based on the liturgies of St. James and the Apostolic Constitutions was a significant achievement. The 1789 American rite did not adopt the Scottish prayer intact, nor the Scottish order for the Celebration of the Holy Communion, but it did adopt a full eucharistic prayer, and in subsequent revisions it improved that prayer by moving the Prayer of Humble Access from a position directly after the Sanctus to one immediately before Communion. The Liturgical Movement of the twentieth century has in general followed the Scottish pattern for the eucharistic prayer in preference to the Roman, although there is now a general consensus that there is no one sequence of themes in the eucharistic prayers that is normative. In this regard the 1979 rite returns to the course of development represented by the 1789 book and abandons the direction (of interpretation, if not of text) which became predominant after the beginning of the Oxford Movement.

The removal of the general intercession from the Celebration of the Holy Communion to the conclusion of the Proclamation of the Word of God is more closely akin to the developed English rite (where it was accounted part of Ante-Communion) than to the Scottish, where it formed the conclusion of the eucharistic prayer. Nevertheless, the contemporary trend is to consider intercession a logical part of the eucharistic prayer as well as of the ministry of the word, and the last portion of some of the new eucharistic prayers (particularly Prayer D) include brief intercessions in the supplication after the invocation.[1]

The eucharistic theology on which the Scottish-American rite is based has also won the day, in its general thrust if not in particular details. The curious synthesis of Calvin, patristic theology, and Eastern Orthodox liturgical tradition provided to the Scottish

Episcopalians a way out of the metaphysical deadlock that made it impossible for most of the Reformers to find a way of articulating the truths which they held about the eucharistic presence and the eucharistic sacrifice. Today, the doctrine of the real presence is generally considered the Anglican position—to so great an extent that present-day Episcopalians seem generally oblivious to the fact that for most of Anglican history this was a very controversial doctrine. The way in which the doctrine is articulated today often bears a strong resemblance to the "virtualist" position of classical Anglicanism that was enshrined in the eucharistic prayers dependent on the Scottish tradition.

As with the doctrine of the real presence, so with the doctrine of the eucharistic sacrifice—the classical Anglican doctrine espoused by Scottish Episcopalians and enshrined in their rite has to a large extent become the standard in the Episcopal Church today. We need to remember that medieval distortions of the doctrine of the eucharistic sacrifice led most of the Reformers to be very wary of the doctrine or to abandon it altogether. The idea that the Eucharist is a representation of Christ's sacrifice before both the Father and the church—an idea which Anglicans came to ground in the Christology of the Epistle to the Hebrews—has come to predominate today in the doctrine of the Eucharist as anamnesis. The Scottish-American rite, unlike English rites in the purer Cranmerian tradition, gives expression to this in the explicit oblation of the bread and wine in the anamnesis of the eucharistic prayer. The American rite of 1979 goes back to the nonjuring roots of this tradition by omitting the so-called "lesser oblation" at the offertory—not found in the nonjuring liturgies that were the precursors of the Scottish rite of 1764 but deriving from the earlier rite of 1637. This "lesser oblation," which directs the celebrant to "offer" the bread and wine when they are prepared as well as during the place where they are offered in the text of the eucharistic prayer, obscures the close bond between the Eucharist as the church's sacrifice and the Eucharist as the anamnesis of Christ's sacrifice and was an unfortunate development.

The 1979 rite developed at a time of remarkable ecumenical consensus on both the shape of the Eucharist and the theology of the Eucharist—a consensus articulated in the various ecumenical documents which we reviewed in the last chapter.

It became apparent in the course of the 1979 revision that to be true to Cranmer's aim of providing a liturgy in the language "understanded of the people", it would be necessary to recast the Eucharist in contemporary language. Rite II succeeds in doing this in a remarkably graceful way. In a way that is still not generally recognized, Cranmer's own rites—a literary masterpiece—work against Cranmer's goals in the twentieth century, because our language has shifted more than we realize. Cranmer and the American revisers of 1789 also both attempted to produce rites which were appropriate for the contemporary pastoral situation in the culture of the day. This work, too, needed redoing in 1979, and the Prayer Book did it successfully. The 1979 Eucharist is a rite which is true to the best of Anglican tradition, articulates this in a way that is congruent to the ecumenical consensus, which has grown out of the Liturgical Movement, and is appropriate to the pastoral situation today.

2. The Unfinished Agenda

The Book of Common Prayer 1979 first went into use in 1976 as the Proposed Book of Common Prayer. It has now been the standard of worship for the Episcopal Church for just more than a decade. It requires a considerable period of time for a church to assimilate a radical revision in its liturgical life. The worship of the English church took more than a century to stabilize after the initial revision in 1549. We need to note, as well, that some of the goals of the Reformation were never successfully achieved—most notably the restoration of the Sunday Eucharist as a weekly communion of the people.

Much of what the 1979 revisers set out to achieve has in fact been assimilated into the life of the church. But there are unfinished agenda as well. Many of these do not relate directly to the Eucharist, but they all have implications for the celebration of the Eucharist as "the epiphany of the Church." These would include the following:

a. Rethinking the Implications of the Initiatory Rites;

b. Rethinking the Implications of the Ministry of the Church articulated in the Initiatory Rites, the Rites for Ordination, and the Catechism;

c. Inclusive Language and the Recovery of a Fuller Use of Biblical Imagery for God;

d. Understanding the Architectural Implications of the Book of Common Prayer 1979;

e. Finding Appropriate Music for Worship;

f. Finding an Appropriate Ceremonial Style;

g. Pruning Extraneous Growth from the "Soft Spots of the Rite";

h. Paying Attention to the Ecumenical Agenda.

Rethinking the Implications of the Initiatory Rites: Holy Baptism is defined by the 1979 Book as "full initiation by water and the Holy Spirit into Christ's Body the Church." The baptized then, whether infants or adults, are entitled to full access to the liturgical life and nurture of the church. Yet until the 1960s the baptized were denied access to Communion until they were confirmed, and recent practice has often been to exclude children altogether from the regular worship of the church, relegating them to informal "Sunday School services" and making worship a predominantly adult affair.

In the 1979 Book children are entitled to access to Communion from the time of Baptism (though this is often delayed by the nonrubrical limitation of first communion to a later age) and the logic of the Prayer Book demands that they be integrated into the regular worship of the church. Aidan Kavanagh writes, with his usual wit:[2]

> Membership in the faithful assembly knows no criteria of age, weight, education, or intelligence quotient—only those of faithful initiation into Christ in his Church. The criteria of faith for sacramental initiation are clear, rigorous, and just; the only criterion of faith after initiation is the living of a life faithful in Christ in his Church. Infants and children may do this in their own way just as well, if not better, than many adults. Be this as it may, the question is not one of the quality or extent of such living but of the rights, acquired through baptism and anointing, to live such a life. Living such a life implies and requires free access at all times to the sacraments of the liturgical assembly. Initiated infants and children may not be adolescents or adults, but they remain fully enfranchised members of the assembly by their sacramental initiation into it, and thus they should be treated as Christians possessing all the rights they are capable of exercising both actively and passively. They have, for example, a right to the assembly's liturgy; they, like other Christians, have no right to anything other than that. The Sunday liturgy is theirs no less than their pastor's or their parents'. And while they will need time and much special help in their growth into full and active participation in that Sunday liturgy, they must neither be nor appear to be disenfranchised of it. Their regular, if not always frequent, attendance at it is

therefore not ideal but normal. If it bores them, it probably bores everyone else as well, and for the same reasons. This counsels that children may well be early and forceful witnesses to liturgical atrophy in their assembly, and that their witness should be taken seriously by all. Children learn much by vigorous ritual engagement, as Erik Erikson has pointed out. They learn perhaps even more by observing what ritual and liturgy do or do not do to adults, especially their parents, and to their peers and siblings. In view of this, children should never regularly be relegated to activities apart from the assembly's liturgy, and special liturgies for children should not so overstimulate them on their own level as to make it hard for them to attend regular Sunday worship, or retard them liturgically on a childish level.

A recent publication of the Episcopal Church's Office of Education for Mission and Ministry, *Children and the Parish Eucharist,* attempts to articulate the implications of this for the Sunday worship of the church. But we are just beginning to work out what all this means. Sunday worship in the Episcopal Church more often than not is still overly rational in its expression and—despite enormous improvement in recent years—less participatory in reality than in intention. Moreover, the treatment of adult baptism as normative (by the design of the Prayer Book rite and in the theology of the rite articulated by liturgical scholars) undercuts the place of baptized children as fully enfranchised members of the church. Recent studies of the theology of baptism in the Armenian and Syriac rites provides an alternative to the Pauline theology and should be explored as a way of articulating the theological significance of the baptism of infants without making adult baptism abnormal.[3]

Related to these issues are issues involved in the sacramental rite which the Prayer Book calls confirmation. Although the Prayer Book itself and the recent revision of the church's canons

CHAPTER SIX:

regarding categories of membership in the church make it clear that the gift bestowed in this rite is strength to live out the mature commitment, which finds expression in a renewal of the baptismal covenant (whether for the first time in confirmation or upon reception into this church or upon reaffirmation at a significant turning point in the life of faith), Episcopalians persist in treating the rite in a way that makes it a puberty rite of "joining the church." It will apparently take considerable time before this rite is used in a way that is consistent with its theology. Doing so is critically important, for mature commitment to Christ is something which the Episcopal Church needs to learn how to foster and articulate.

The church has made a tentative beginning in all of this. The baptismal liturgy is restored to the Sunday Eucharist, with further preference indicated for baptismal feasts—Easter, Pentecost, the Baptism of Christ, All Saints' Day or Sunday, and the bishop's visitation. Most parishes seem to have made a conscientious attempt to put these rubrics into practice. Rites drafted by the Standing Liturgical Commission under the title "The Preparation of Parents and Godparents for the Baptism of Infants and Young Children" are designed to serve as the liturgical component of a program parallel to the catechumenate, which will deepen the Christian formation of those who will present infants or young children for Baptism. When conscientiously followed, they should create an appropriate setting for the formation of the children who are to be baptized and serve as a safeguard against indiscriminate baptism.

The recent revision of the canons regarding categories of membership brings the church's legislation into conformity with its liturgy. *The Book of Occasional Services* provides rites for a catechumenate, and efforts are being made to put these provisions into systematic use, though the catechumenate is not yet common and the provisions have frequently been used for Confirmation rather than for Baptism in a way that undermines the integrity of the theology that underlies them. The Standing Liturgical Commission has now prepared rites for "Preparation of Baptized Persons for Reaffirmation of the Baptismal Covenant" parallel to the rites for the catechumenate which are the liturgical component of a program designed to foster the mature commitment spoken of in the "confirmation" rites. The success of such programs where they have been tried should commend them to the church at large as it seeks to replace the inherited patterns of Christian formation which have proved inadequate for the needs of the church in the present age.

Rethinking the Implications of the Ministry of the Church: The 1979 Book is very clear that ministry is a responsibility to which we are called by Baptism and that the ordained ministries of the church are not three variants of priesthood but separate and distinct orders. The clear designation of appropriate roles in the worship of the church is a step in this direction. The vesture of candidates for ordination to the presbyterate and the episcopate (alb, surplice, or rochet, without insignia of rank or order) is a ritual statement that it is Baptism, and not prior ordination to a "lower" order, that qualifies those candidates. The church is struggling to recover a genuine diaconal ministry in what is generally called the "vocational" diaconate.

Yet the very words which we use obscure our meaning. Talk of the laity as a fourth order of ministry (cf. the Catechism) obscures the vision of the church as the people (laos) of God, to which ordained and nonordained alike belong and whose responsibilities both share. It is more accurate theologically to speak of the ordained as having particular ministries besides those which they share with other Christians by virtue of baptism than to speak of "laity" as another order of ministry.

168

Besides this, "minister" and "ministry" are such clericalized words in our vocabulary that "lay ministers" are perhaps more generally perceived as "clericalized" lay persons than as persons exercising the responsibilities to which they were called by Baptism. We would probably do better to cease to use the word "ministry" and replace it with the word "service"—what we are really talking about here is Christian service to God and to the world in God's Name. The cluster of ideas and phrases associated with "minister" inevitably bring to mind the perspective with which the church has worked for more than a millenium, of a church in which the ordained minister to the nonordained, rather than the authentic biblical perspective in which the church as a whole ministers to the world and the ordained are charged with helping equip the church for this service.

A recent evolution within the church's perspective on its ministry has been the realization that the restriction of ordination to males is a cultural and sociological limitation on ministry that is not grounded in the Gospel itself. As a consequence of its discovery that Paul numbered women among his colleagues in his ministry and that women played an important role among the disciples of Jesus, and of the insight that the distinction of male and female has no bearing on one's place in the life of the church (cf. Galatians), the Episcopal Church has now ordained women to the diaconate and the presbyterate and has removed canonical bars to their ordination to the episcopate.

While these decisions seem to have general support in the church as a whole, it cannot be said that there is unanimous consensus about them, for there are still those who are reluctant to accept the ministrations of ordained women, and the consecration of the first woman as bishop is certain to be a matter of considerable controversy.

Inclusive Language and Imagery for God: The drafters of the 1979 Book became increasingly aware in the course of revision that theological integrity made it mandatory that they use language that was unambiguously inclusive when referring to both men and women. A similar concern was widespread in contemporary society and may be seen in guidelines issued by the National Council of Teachers of English. In the liturgical texts, it meant care with such words as "man" or "men," "brothers," and "sons" and with the use of pronouns. On the whole, the drafters accomplished this task with grace and skill—exceptions are found only in occasional texts from Rite I, in direct citations of authorized translations of Scripture, in the psalter, and—surprisingly—in the Burial Office (the place where the language seemed incongruous even before inclusive language became a generally recognized issue). A similar concern was before the drafters of *The Hymnal 1982,* although their task was in many ways more difficult, because they were dealing with poetic texts. At present, it is primarily in the versions of the Bible authorized for use in public worship that this issue arises in the church's liturgy.

A related issue arises from the theological truth that God transcends the distinction of gender and embraces the masculine and the feminine alike in the divine nature. This is a knottier problem to wrestle with, for it makes the use of any third-person pronoun for God problematic. Our liturgical texts offend more than the Scriptures themselves in one part of this problem: the Scriptures do not hesitate to use feminine imagery and metaphors for God from time to time, while the imagery and metaphors of the Prayer Book are at present exclusively masculine when they are gender-specific. The church is now in the process of trying to produce graceful rites which take these issues into account. The process has only just begun, and it is likely to be some time before the problem is resolved successfully. It is difficult, when we have only just settled into the use of a new rite, to contemplate further

170

revision, but revision is in reality a never-ending process, and the issues of inclusive language and the language which we use for God must be taken into account as the church looks to the future.

Architectural Implications: We noted in the last chapter the architectural implications of the present rite, and in earlier chapters we noted the ways in which the church tried to design buildings appropriate to worship before the Gothic revival swept before it. It is one thing to design new buildings with the requirements of the Book of Common Prayer 1979 in mind; it is a far more difficult task to redesign, in ways that are stylistically appropriate, the buildings which we already have. Nevertheless, if revision of our liturgical space is not undertaken, new rites will not "work" in the way they are intended to "work." Just as medieval buildings had to be redesigned at the Reformation for the use of the Book of Common Prayer, so our present, often neomedieval buildings will need to be redesigned. This is a pastorally sensitive task, for on the whole we still tend to favor the "numinous atmosphere" which Gothic buildings create, and sensitive change requires considerable skill. Another dimension of this task is the design of baptistries suitable for the baptism of adults. While we will continue to baptize infants and children, the Prayer Book gives the baptism of adults at least equivalent status (the rubrics of the present rite would seem to make it normative), and baptistries designed (as most of ours are) in such a way as to make adult baptism abnormal contradict the theology which the Prayer Book articulates.

Music: It has been said the Episcopal Prayer Books provide a said Eucharist which may be sung, while the Lutheran Book of Worship provides a sung rite which may be said. There is a considerable amount of historical truth in this. Although Merbecke provided a setting for the 1549 Eucharist, he did not revise his setting for the 1552 rite, and it was the Daily Office that received musical attention in the early centuries of Anglican worship. Only with the Oxford Movement did choral settings for the Eucharist once again become widespread, and even at that it seems to have been "said mass" at early services and on weekdays that had the decisive impact on Episcopal piety. Besides this, for most of its history Anglican worship has had for hymnody a rather sterile tradition of metrical psalmody, unlike the rich hymnody of the Lutheran churches. It was not until the nineteenth century that Anglicanism enriched its tradition of hymnody from other sources. The musical tradition of Anglicanism is thus relatively recent and also reveals a bias toward choir music (in the cathedral tradition) rather than congregational singing.

The recovery of an appropriate musical setting for the Sunday Eucharist today is not made easier by the fact that we live in a culture which has lost a tradition of community singing and has also made music a stepchild in public education. Musicians thus work against considerable odds in seeking to make a sung Eucharist with active congregational participation the norm for parish worship. The Standing Commission on Church Music and the Church Hymnal Corporation have nevertheless done their best to provide appropriate musical resources for the Book of Common Prayer 1979. Greater use of cantors, careful use of the choir so that it supports rather than supplants congregational singing, thoughtful work at building a congregation's repertoire of hymnody and service music, and careful training are essential if the musical goals of the 1979 rite are to be achieved.

The Ceremonial Setting: One result of the success of the Oxford Movement was the uncritical appropriation of the ceremonial tradition of the Roman rite in Episcopal worship. So widespread did this become, that even a low-church style of celebration came to reflect Roman ceremonial practices in ways that became so common as to be unrecognizable as Roman in origin by most

Episcopalians. At present, Episcopalians seem to oscillate between uncritical imitation of a medieval Roman past and trendy use of contemporary gimmickry. The author has argued elsewhere (in *Prayer Book Rubrics Expanded*) for a ceremonial usage which is appropriate to the liturgical insights of the present day and true to the best of Anglican tradition.

Remaining Soft Spots: We noted in the last chapter the "soft spots" in the Eucharist, which have historically attracted "clutter" that distorts the shape of the rite—the Entrance, the Offertory, and the Communion and Dismissal. The 1979 Book deals least successfully with the entrance. The Canadian *Book of Alternative Services* comments in the rationale for its eucharistic rite that the Prayer Book has remnants of no less than seven distinct entrance rites. The author can find only six in ours—an entrance psalm, a hymn before the service, prayers from the celebrant's private preparation (the Collect for Purity), the penitential preparation represented by the farced Kyrie, the Gloria in excelsis as a bridge canticle between the office and the Eucharist (cf. Juan Mateos), and the Kyrie as the remnant of an entrance litany. The 1979 rubrics allow a good deal of flexibility at the entrance, but in practice we still devote a disproportionate amount of time to getting started. Especially in said services, there seems to be no good reason why the service should not begin at once with a greeting or acclamation and the collect of the day; and at sung services, it would seem appropriate to have one entrance song, whether that be psalm, hymn, or canticle.

The rubrical provisions for the offertory in the 1979 rite are clean enough, but the temptation to use a presentation hymn or sentence seems too great for most to resist, and it is not uncommon to see the offertory cluttered with other prayers and with complicated and distracting ceremonial actions (such as the elevation of the alms basin and even the singing of patriotic songs and movement of flags!). The Communion and dismissal is often "dragged out" by obtrusive ways of doing practical things (the ablutions and extinguishing the candles), a hymn added *after* the assembly has been dismissed, and "concluding" prayers or devotions added after the dismissal as well. We need to be conscientious in avoiding or even pruning back the growth of clutter in all these places.

The Ecumenical Agenda: "Interim Eucharistic Sharing" between Lutherans and Episcopalians and concelebrations with ministers of other traditions of the 1984 COCU and the Lima rites are canonical possibilities at present. Growing consensus about eucharistic theology makes this possible, and the scandal of a divided church should press us toward more frequent use of these provisions as a way of growth into the unity which Christ wills for the church. Certain cautions are in order in such situations, however. Our own theological integrity should lead us to press for a full eucharistic prayer when the Eucharist is celebrated according to the Lutheran Book of Worship. In joint celebrations with other churches, the COCU rite is probably to be preferred to that of Lima, which has a certain incoherence in its structure (an entrance litany *and* a litanic form of the Prayers of the People; a eucharistic prayer with a double epiclesis) and a certain preciousness in its preference for foreign phrases in the people's responses (Veni Creator Spiritus and Maranatha as well as Kyrie eleison). The Lima rite shows some of the defects that may occur in hybrid rites which borrow elements from different traditions without integrating them into a new synthesis.

3. Future Agenda: The Church and Society

In the sections that follow we turn our attention to areas which at first do not seem directly related to the Eucharist: (1) the church and society and (2) the broader theological context. In actual fact, when the eucharistic assembly is understood as "the epiphany of the church," these broader issues are brought to focus in the church's celebration of the Eucharist, and it is important to see the reverberations that these areas have in the church's worship.

Robert Bruce Mullin argues persuasively in *Episcopal Vision/ American Reality* that, through Bishop Hobart and others, the church before the Oxford Movement understood itself as an alternative to the predominantly revivalist character of other denominations. Its emphasis was not on sudden conversion but on steady growth and nurture in the Christian faith. Though not an established church, it tended to function as the church of the established order.

It developed a close and at times idolatrous identification with the cause of American democracy—often revealed in the habit of placing an American flag in the chancel. This close connection with American culture meant that the Episcopal Church tended to stand on the sidelines during the Civil War. The twentieth century saw the rise of leaders, who—unlike nineteenth-century Episcopalians—were willing to give the moral integrity of the church and its fidelity to the Gospel priority over the peace of the church and its position in American society. The resulting turmoil undermined at least in part, however, the church's self-identity: when forced to choose between God and country, most Americans choose country or look for a religious tradition which disguises any conflicts between the two. The decision to place the church's moral authority at stake on the issue of civil rights in the 1960s and 1970s was courageous but costly.

Most "mainline" denominations made the same decision. In a curious reversal of roles, the classic churches of the Reformation, which had historically been captives of the predominant culture, cast off their bonds in fidelity to the Gospel, while those newer denominations, which historically advocated strict separation from the world, became the champions of the "American way." The watershed here is the recent decision of Southern Baptists, historically the fiercest proponents of separation of church and state, to enter the political arena as "the moral majority."

While all of this may seem unrelated to the celebration of the Eucharist, it has more bearing than is immediately apparent. The older symbiotic relation between church and state found expression in the way that prayers for those in civil authority were worded: those in authority in medieval and Reformation society in England had been understood as the leaders of Christian society, and until 1979 prayers for "Christian" rulers were still incorporated in the Prayer for the Whole State of Christ's *Church."* Flags carried in the Sunday procession and patriotic songs at the offertory (with which they had no theological relation at all) tended to blur the boundaries between church and state in a very dangerous way.

The revision of intercessions for civil authorities at the Sunday Eucharist and the removal of inappropriate patriotic hymns and symbols carried a message that did not go unnoticed and was not popular. The use of the Eucharist as an act of protest or political witness (as in "peace masses" outside the Pentagon and elsewhere) was a dubious use of the dubious tradition of votive masses which exacerbated the conflict.

Nevertheless, the Christ whose sacrifice is represented in the eucharistic memorial is a redeemer who liberates us from the forces of oppression, and while the Eucharist ought not to be used as a political statement, it gives expression to a Gospel which does have political consequences. While the nuances of liberation theology may distort the perspective of the Gospel, such theology is a legitimate protest against the cultural captivity of the church. And that cultural captivity is nowhere more diabolical than in fundamentalist churches where patriotic self-interest is disguised in the garments of evangelical truth.

Future Agenda: The Theological Context

The revision of the Book of Common Prayer brought a fundamental realignment of the traditional "parties" in the Episcopal Church. The theological convergence which finds expression in the 1979 Eucharist meant that both Catholic tradition and Reformation principles found clearer expression there than they had in any prior Anglican rite. The eucharistic rite, moreover, represents a genuine theological synthesis rather than a compromise, so that neither Catholics nor Evangelicals gained at the expense of others.

For this reason the traditional "parties" in the church simply collapsed. The American Church Union, the organized voice of the Catholic position for much of the twentieth century, simply disintegrated during the course of prayer book revision. Its legitimate liturgical goals had been achieved. "Low-church" and "high-church" were reabsorbed into "central Anglicanism" (as was generally true in the United States before the 1830s). Only the extremes at the two ends of the theological spectrum held out . . . , and they did so out of convictions which were at times only partly theological. In fact, they made common cause in such movements as the Evangelical and Catholic Mission and the Society for the Preservation of the Book of Common Prayer. In both cases their opposition was grounded in the perception that the Book of Common Prayer 1979 represented a theological shift. The theological shift, which was in fact real, was rooted in the theological understanding of the relation of church to culture.

The root issue theologically is determining to what extent the "setting" of biblical literature is social context and to what extent it is revealed content: it is an issue of biblical interpretation. Are the social and political norms of the society in which Jesus and Paul worked divinely ordained, or are they human institutions which we must rethink in the light of the Gospel? In particular, this issue manifests itself in the question of whether a patriarchal structure is normative for Christian life and ethics and whether the political order is divinely ordained or of human origin. In the cultural convulsions of the 1960s and 1970s, the Episcopal Church, by endorsing the ordination of women, challenged the patriarchal norm of much of biblical society (where men held the significant power). More recently the church has engaged in a reexamination of the normative roles of men and women within marriage and in society at large and the normative character of marriage as the sole context for sexual intimacy. This challenge to traditional patriarchal norms has troubled both Catholic and Evangelical traditionalists. The moral critique of society on issues of civil rights, social justice, international order, and human rights also troubled these groups.

These are in fact serious issues, and they have created fault lines in the Christian churches which differ from the older Catholic-Protestant divisions. In the eyes of traditionalists, the radical position on these issues represents a secular rejection of biblical norms. The radical position sees itself, however, as grounded in the radical character of the Gospel itself, which does indeed relativize the normative character of the social order in which the biblical narrative is set. Women were in fact prominent among the followers of Jesus during his ministry and did in fact play an active role in the ministry of the early church, as is evident in the Pauline literature. The relegation of women to subordinate status in the church, as seen in the pastoral epistles, can be understood as the church's capitulation to the patriarchal culture of the day.

In a similar way, both the sayings of Jesus and the rulings of Paul relativize marriage as a social norm, while elevating the status of women within marriage. Both Jesus and Paul, for example, commend those who would remain unmarried "for the sake of the kingdom"; Jesus protests against the one-sided right of men to divorce their wives; and Paul discusses conflicts of faith which may be grounds for divorce. Whether one understands the subordination of women as part of the created order or as a consequence of the fall depends on how one reads the Genesis narratives (in the first creation story, God creates humanity "male and female"; in the second story, the prior creation of man is sometimes understood to justify the subordinate position of women). And gay and lesbian relationships, premarital sexual intimacy, contraception, and abortion raise complex issues which biblical texts simply do not directly address or else do not provide definitive answers to.

Biblical texts likewise reveal a wide spectrum of approaches to the political order—the attitude of Paul toward the established political order is very different, for example, from that of the author of the Book of Revelation. It is therefore very difficult to present any of these approaches as normative, and down through the ages the churches have constantly shifted in their assessment of the proper relationship between the church and the civil order.

A deeper theological question concerns the very nature of God. Those who claim that God transcends the distinction of gender have the witness of both Genesis 1 and Galatians on their side, and the not insignificant use of feminine imagery for God would seem to preclude ascribing to God an exclusively masculine nature. In this regard, popular Christian tradition is narrower than the biblical witness, although neither biblical Hebrew nor contemporary English make it easy to speak of God without ascribing to God a grammatical gender.

Another theological issue is found in the theology of prayer implicit in evangelical and charismatic practice. Theologically, prayer is the expression of our commitment to be "honest to God" about our desires and concerns, an effort to conform our will to the sovereign will and purposes of God, and a pledge to work for the accomplishment of God's purposes. We pray in the conviction that God hears and uses our prayer. But evangelical and charismatic Christians do not always avoid the danger of slipping unconsciously into a position of telling God what to do and of hoping to conform God's will to ours in a way that becomes manipulative and idolatrous.

Another theological fault line is found in the contrast between a revivalist theology, which plays on human emotions in its appeal for conversion, and a more balanced faith which does not sacrifice the gift of reason on the altar of an irrational God. The Episcopal Church has always taken reason as well as Scripture, tradition, and experience into account in its worship as well as its theology, and laid greater stress on nurture than on conversion. Revivals wax and wane, and without an emphasis on steady nurture conversion has little staying power or long-term impact on our lives. But the deep-rooted nature of human sin also means that conversion is a necessity in the Christian life, and that without continuous conversion our faith grows weak. We cannot abandon our emphasis on steady nurture, but we must never forget the need for conversion either.

The Coming Years

The issues facing the Episcopal Church are not insignificant, and the prospects for conflict are very real. This conflict will find expression in our worship because the revision of our liturgical texts has made worship reflect far more directly the actual life of Episcopalians than was true at a time when the language of worship made it a kind of refuge from the realities of life in the world.

We are in the process of radically reshaping our identity— partly out of the insights gained in our present liturgical life and partly out of conscientious theological and moral conviction. Our older identity was much like that espoused by John Henry Hobart. We saw our religious life as being essentially harmonious with the ideals of American society. The new identity which is emerging is to some extent countercultural and stands over against contemporary American society. For me, this newer identity is the only one which is possible for us if we are to retain our theological integrity. But this newer identity is not necessarily a popular one, and the shift in identity is one of the reasons for the present conflict in the life of the church. The older identity was one that most people found much more comfortable.

A proverb makes a curse of the expression "May you live in interesting times." There is little doubt that times will be interesting for the Episcopal Church as it wrestles with some of the issues which we have just reviewed. I close with the conviction that our worship, and in particular the Eucharist of the 1979 Book of Common Prayer, provides us with the resources to be faithful to God in the interesting times that are coming.

Notes to Chapter Six

BIBLIOGRAPHICAL NOTES

By its very nature, the assessments of the present situation and the future agenda are a personal evaluation and do not readily lend themselves to bibliographical reference. As the earlier chapters of this book reveal, our perspective on the past shifts from age to age; contemporary history by its very nature is an even more inexact discipline. The first section of this chapter is a brief review of the first five chapters of this book, whose bibliographical notes should be consulted. Important references for topics not treated at length earlier in this work are listed below.

There is an extensive literature at present on the initiatiory rites and their implications for the life of the church. Aidan Kavanagh, *The Shape of Baptism* (New York, Pueblo, 1978) is a good summary of the state of the question at the time when the Book of Common Prayer 1979 was adopted and also presents the background for the restoration of the catechumenate. Daniel Stevick, *Baptismal Moments, Baptismal Meanings* (New York, Church Hymnal Corporation, 1988) is an excellent discussion of the current state of the question in the Episcopal Church. The authorized rites for the catechumenate in the Episcopal Church are found in *The Book of Occasional Services* (New York, Church Hymnal Corporation, 1979). The parallel rites referred to in this chapter will also be published by the Church Hymnal Corporation for the Standing Liturgical Commission. The theology of infant baptism is explored by Mark Searle in his article "Infant Baptism Reconsidered" in a collection of essays which he edited, *Alternate Futures for Worship, Volume 2: Baptism and Confirmation* (Collegeville, MN, Liturgical Press, 1987). Gabriele Winkler's important work on baptism in the Armenian rite, *Das armenische Initiationsrituale* (Rome, Orientalia Christiana Analecta, 1982) is unfortunately not available in English.

There is an extensive bibliography on the ministry of the church. Two key books in the current discussion are Eduard Schillebeecx, *Ministry* (New York, Crossroads, 1981) and Bernard Cooke, *Ministry to Word and Sacraments* (Philadelphia, Fortress, 1980). The works of the early twentieth-century Anglican missionary Roland Allen have had a profound impact on contemporary thought about ministry. It is, however, far from certain that the patterns and models appropriate in the missionary situation in which Allen worked are appropriate to contemporary American society. Anne Rowthorn, *The Liberation of the Laity* (Wilton, CT, Morehouse-Barlow, 1987) is one author who attempts to apply them, and similar insights of liberation theologians from Latin American, to the present situation of the Episcopal Church. A good introduction to the restoration of a functional diaconate is James Monroe Barnett, *The Diaconate, A Full and Equal Order* (New York, Seabury, 1981).

The bibliography for inclusive language is also extensive. The hermeneutical background is explored by Elizabeth Schuessler-Fiorenza in two books, *Bread, Not Stone* (Boston, Beacon Press, 1984) and *In Memory of Her* (New York, Crossroads, 1983). The issue of liturgical language receives careful treatment by Gail Ramshaw-Schmidt in *Christ and Sacred Speech* (Philadelphia, Fortress, 1986). A thoughtful discussion of the use of both masculine and feminine imagery for God (rather than the elimination of gender-specific imagery) is found in an article by Robert L. Hurd entitled "Complementarity" in *Worship* (vol. 61, no. 5, September 1987).

For other topics covered in this chapter (such as the ecumenical context, the architectural setting, and theological issues) relevant works are cited in earlier

CHAPTER SIX:

chapters. The *Companion* to the Hymnal 1982, in preparation by the Church Hymnal Corporation under Raymond F. Glover as general editor, will be an important resource on music when it is published.

NOTES ON THE TEXT

1. Cf. Kenneth Stevenson, *Eucharist and Offering,* page 226. This trend cannot yet be said to represent a general consensus. Many liturgists would wish to restrict the scope of anaphoral intercessions, lest intercessions in the text of the Great Thanksgiving, which is the celebrant's prayer, erode the active inclusion of the congregation in the ministry of intercession as this finds expression in the Prayers of the People. Historically, it was the development of anaphoral intercession that led to the disappearance of the Prayers of the People in the West.

2. Aidan Kavanagh, OSB, *Elements of Rite* (New York, Pueblo, 1982), pages 67–68. *Children and the Parish Eucharist* begins with this quote.

3. The words "norm" and "normative" may be understood in different ways. The logic of printing the rite for adult baptism as the model in the Book of Common Prayer and making rubrical provision for changes necessary when the rite is used for baptism of infants would seem to indicate that adult baptism is the norm. Aidan Kavanagh in *The Shape of Baptism* (pages 109–115) treats adult baptism as the norm, but defines "norm" in such as way as to speak of the "abnormality" of infant baptism, while acknowledging that "tradition seems to know the baptism of infants from the beginning" and that infant baptism is "a benign abnormality so long as it is practiced with prudence." He does not advocate denying baptism of infants which results from "the frail health of the infant" or "the earnest desire of Christian parents whose faith is vigorous and whose way of life gives clear promise that their child will develop in the faith of the church." However, I would wish to differ from him in considering the baptism of infants of practicing and committed Christian parents as normative and not "abnormal" in any sense of the word.

Theological and Liturgical Terms

1. Theology of the Eucharistic Presence

Accidents
the outward appearances of a substance; in the doctrine of transubstantiation the accidents of bread and wine remain after the consecration at the Eucharist, but the substance is transformed into the body and blood of Christ.

Consecration
the setting apart of something for religious use; in the Eucharist, the setting apart of bread and wine so that they become sacramentally the body and blood of Christ (or, in receptionist doctrine, so that they become the instruments by which the communicant receives the body and blood of Christ).

Consusbstantiation
the doctrine which holds that the substance of the body and blood of Christ is given "in, with, and under" the substance of the bread and wine. Lutherans, who hold this doctrine, did not themselves apply this term to it and have not always been comfortable with it.

Memorialism
Zwingli's doctrine of the Eucharist, which holds that Christ is present to the memory of the worshiper at the Lord's Supper.

Oblation	something offered or the act of offering something—a synonym for "offering." In Cranmer's eucharistic prayer, Christ is said to have made an "oblation" of himself on the cross for the sins of the whole world. The "oblations" made by the worshipers at the Eucharist may be either money offerings (the original sense of the word in the Prayer for the Whole State of Christ's Church) or the bread and wine (the sense in which it was understood in this prayer in the 1928 American rite). Ceremonially, Anglicans have spoken of a "lesser oblation" of the bread and wine when they are prepared at the offertory and of their oblation in the course of the eucharistic prayer (in the paragraph following the Institution Narrative in Scottish American Rites). Luther disliked talk of oblation and offering at the Eucharist, for he felt that it undercut the Pauline doctrine of justification by grace. The last portion of Cranmer's 1549 eucharistic prayer articulates the self-oblation of the worshiper; in 1552 this was detached and made an alternative postcommunion prayer.
Offering	See oblation. In addition, this term is generally used for the alms given at a service.
Propitiation	placating [God]. Reformers repudiated the idea of the Eucharist as a propitiatory sacrifice which could effect our reconciliation with God.
Real Presence	a term that has been variously defined, depending on the meaning of "real." (1) In the broadest definition, it means the "true" presence. When Dix characterizes Zwingli's doctrine as one which sets forth a "real absence," he is abusing this meaning of the term. (2) In a more restricted sense, it means the "objective" presence of Christ and emphasizes that Christ's presence is not dependent on the subjective faith of the worshiper. (3) In the strict philosophical sense of the term, it means the presence of the "res" of the sacrament, and can properly be applied only to

those doctrines which hold that the substance of Christ's body and blood are present in the bread and wine. The Black Rubric of the 1559 Book of Common Prayer denies the real presence in the third but not the second sense of the term, as may be seen in the alteration in the wording of the rubric when it was restored in 1662. William Nicholson carefully sets out the meaning of the term in the quotation found in chapter 1.

Receptionism   the doctrine espoused by Richard Hooker and Daniel Waterland, among others, which holds that Christ's body and blood are present to the communicant in receiving Communion, so that the bread and wine instrumentally effect Christ's presence to the believer. In this doctrine, Christ is present to the believer, but not "in" the bread and wine.

Representation   a word with a stronger and a weaker sense in theological vocabulary. In the stronger sense, Christ is sacramentally "re-presented" or made present in the Eucharist. In the weaker sense, to represent means to stand for something which is absent.

Sacrifice   a term of widely varied and often disputed meaning. In a general sense, it means a "costly offering" to God. Whether or not the Eucharist could properly be called a sacrifice, and if so in what sense, was a matter of intense dispute and sometimes acrimonious debate at the Reformation.

Suppletory Sacrifice   a sacrifice which "completes" Christ's sacrifice on the cross. Reformers consistently denied that the Eucharist could "add" anything to what Christ has done for us on the cross.

Substance   the inner reality of something, as contrasted to its outward appearance. Cf. transubstantiation.

Transubstantiation   the doctrine officially held by the Roman Catholic Church, which affirms that at the Eucharist the substance of the bread and wine is transformed through consecration into the body and blood of Christ, though the "accidents" of the bread and wine remain.

Ubiquity
the omnipresence of the glorified body of Christ. Luther used this doctrine to explain how Christ could be present in the bread and wine of the Eucharist.

Virtualism
the doctrine found in the *Institutes* of Calvin and espoused by John Johnson, many Nonjurors, and Samuel Seabury, which holds that Christ is present in the sacrament by the power ("virtue") of the Spirit.

2. Theology of the Eucharistic Sacrifice

Anamnesis
the act of remembrance in prayer and ritual action by which a past reality is made present and efficacious in the present. This use of the Greek word (found in the biblical command, "Do this in *remembrance* of me") is a contemporary one which refers to the "re-presentation" of Christ's saving actions in the Eucharist.

Eucharistic Sacrifice
literally, "a sacrifice of thanksgiving." In this sense, it refers to the offering of thanks to God in the Great Thanksgiving of the Eucharist. In a broader sense, it refers to the Eucharist as a sacrifice in other ways (which must be spelled out by the person using the term).

Impetrative Sacrifice
a sacrifice which pleads or entreats ("impetrates") the favor toward the offerer of the one to whom the sacrifice is offered.

3. General Theological Terms

Anglo-Catholic
"English Catholic," a term first used in the nineteenth century in the Oxford Movement to desig-

nate doctrine and liturgical practice conforming to that of the undivided church of the early centuries, or one who upholds such doctrine and practice. In reality, Anglo-Catholics have generally been more influenced than they recognize or admit by Roman Catholic standards established by the Council of Trent.

Arian

one who denies the full divinity of Jesus Christ. The term is derived from the name of Arius, a third-century presbyter of Alexandria who taught this position, which was repudiated by the Church at the Council of Nicaea.

Arminian

one who repudiates the Calvinist doctrine of absolute predestination. The term is derived from the name of Arminius (Jakob Hermandszoon), a seventeenth-century Dutch theologian who took this position. It was loosely applied to English Christians who took a similar position, and at times used as a label for the Laudian school in the Church of England.

Calvinist

one who adheres to the position of John Calvin, in whole or in part. The keystone of Calvin's theological system was the doctrine of election; many who did not hold his doctrine of election did hold to his eucharistic doctrine, which has been labeled "virtualist." See the Appended Note to Chapter 1.

Churchman

a term originally coined to describe one who supported the ministry, the liturgy, the theology, and the traditions and usages of the Church of England as established by law, as contrasted to those who dissented from them or wished to "purify" them. By the late seventeenth century "high-churchman" was used as a term for this position, and "low-churchman" and "broad-churchman" were later coined on the same model for other positions. They are imprecise as descriptive terms. Liturgically, they generally designate today the degree to which one adheres to the traditions of the pre-Reformation Church. Theologically, "high-church" generally designates today an emphasis on the continuity of Anglicanism with the traditions of Catholic Christendom, while "low-church" designates an emphasis on solidarity with the Continental Reformation, and "broad-church" designates a broad interpretation of doctrinal orthodoxy and liturgical practice which finds a place for both. Historically, "low-church" was first applied in the eighteenth century to the Latitudinarians and then in the nineteenth century to the Evangelicals—two very different groups of Anglicans. "Broadchurch" came into use in the nineteenth century and in the United States was used for the "Evangelical Catholicism" of William Augustus Muhlenberg and his followers.

Deist a term generally used for one who holds a belief in a God who is creator but is remote from the world after creation and uninvolved with it.

Election the Calvinist doctrine, based on Romans 8 and other passages, that God elects or chooses some for salvation on the basis of God's sovereign freedom without any reference to human merit.

Evangelical "grounded in the Gospel"—a term for those who place strong emphasis on the Gospel as the basis for Christian life and practice and less emphasis on tradition and reason as standards of authority. On the Continent, "Evangelical" is generally used in preference to the term "Protestant." The Evangelicals in Anglicanism have traditionally placed greater emphasis on solidarity with the continental churches of the Reformation and less emphasis on Anglican continuity with pre-Reformation Catholic tradition.

Latitudinarian the term "latitude-men" was originally given to the Cambridge Platonists, for whom reason was the "candle of the Lord" and who gave broad scope to reason and advocated a broad interpretation of the standards of orthodoxy. As reason became more narrowly defined in the era of the Enlightenment, the liberal views of the Latitudinarians often departed from biblical and creedal orthodoxy.

Laudian

a name loosely given to the follows of William Laud, Archbishop of Canterbury in the reign of Charles I and an articulate "high-churchman" in the late seventeenth-century sense of that word. Laud also repudiated the doctrine of absolute predestination and for that reason he and his followers were sometimes labeled Arminians.

Nonjuror

one who declined to take the oath of allegiance to William and Mary after James II was removed in 1688. No bishop of the Church of Scotland was willing to take this oath, and Scottish Episcopalians eventually formed a separate church.

Predestination

the Calvinist doctrine that those whom God has chosen or elected are predestined for salvation. In its absolute form this doctrine also asserts that those predestined for salvation cannot fall from grace, and that those not predestined for salvation are predestined by God for damnation ("double predestination").

Puritan

a term for English Calvinists from the Reformation to the Restoration. They generally wished to "purify" the liturgy of the church, removing all practices for which they could find no explicit scriptural warrant. Many, but not all, also wished to reform the organization of the Church of England along Genevan lines. They generally conformed to the Church of England until the time of the Restoration; during the Commonwealth they overthrew the established liturgy and the episcopacy and imposed the doctrinal standards of the Westminster Confession and the liturgical standards of the Westminster Directory on the Church. In Virginia, early Puritans eventually conformed to Anglican usages. In New England,

Puritans succeeded in establishing churches and worshiping along Genevan lines, although they generally considered themselves members of the Church of England (the Pilgrims who settled in Plymouth were an exception in this regard). See the Appended Note to Chapter 1.

Socinian

one who denies the divinity of Jesus Christ. The term is derived from the name of Fausto Sozzini, an Italian reformer who held this position and found a strong following in Poland.

Trent

the Council which reformed the Roman Catholic Church in the late sixteenth century in response to medieval abuses and in reaction to the Reformation.

Tridentine

an adjective derived from "Trent." See Trent.

Unitarian

one who rejects the orthodox doctrine of the Trinity, denying the divinity of Jesus Christ and of the Holy Spirit. Some Anglicans held Unitarian views, but a fixed liturgy, the liturgical use of the Creeds, and episcopal polity preserved Trinitarian orthodoxy in Anglicanism (King's Chapel in Boston, however, became Unitarian after the Revolution). Unitarian views found favor in the seventeenth century among English Presbyterians, and New England Congregationalism moved toward Unitarianism in the late seventeenth and eighteenth centuries. Early Unitarians were often known as Arians or Socinians. Earlier English and American Unitarianism was scriptural in its formulation; later it came under the influence of rationalism.

Zwinglian

a follower of Ulrich Zwingli, an early Swiss Reformer in Zurich. His doctrine was generally similar to that of Calvin, but he held a less objective view of the presence of Christ in the Eucharist. His eucharistic doctrine has sometimes been unfairly characterized as upholding the "real absence" of Christ at the Eucharist. See Memorialism.

4. General Liturgical Terms

Acclamation

a phrase "cried out" in worship. In the 1979 Eucharist, the "Opening Acclamation" is "Blessed be God . . ." or its seasonal variant; the "memorial acclamation" in the course of Eucharistic Prayer A, B, and D is the people's response which comes sometime after the Institution Narrative. Eucharistic Prayer C has frequent acclamations or responses for the people.

Agnus Dei

the anthem, "O Lamb of God . . ." which was originally introduced to be sung during the fraction or breaking of the bread. It is frequently used as a communion rather than a fraction anthem.

Alms

offerings for the charitable work of the church.

Altar

strictly defined, the place of sacrifice. This term is frequently used for the table where the Eucharist is celebrated; its use is often avoided by those who deny a sacrificial interpretation for the Eucharist and "holy table" or a similar term used in its place.

Anamnesis

remembrance. In the Great Thanksgiving, this term designates the paragraph following the Institution Narrative which affirms the church's intention to offer the Eucharist "in remembrance" of Christ according to his commandment at the Last Supper.

Anaphora

offering—the Greek name for the Great Thanksgiving.

Ante-Communion

an Anglican term for the Proclamation of the Word of God, when this is not followed by the Celebration of the Holy Communion. In English usage, it includes the Prayer for the Whole State of Christ's Church; since 1789 in American usage it has ended with the Gospel [and Sermon].

Benedictus qui venit	"Blessed is he who comes in the name of the Lord"—a phrase generally added at the end of the Sanctus but deleted by Cranmer in 1552. Its original sense in this context is probably a reference to Christ's coming in the incarnation; its deletion arises from the fact that many have interpreted it as referring to Christ's coming to us in Communion.
Blessing	a term used to designate the prayer of a bishop or presbyter asking God's blessing on the congregation at the end of the Eucharist.
Canon	an ecclesiastical rule or law. It has a variety of meanings; liturgically, it refers to the eucharistic prayer as established by the church's rule. Properly speaking, the "canon [gratiarum] actionis" begins with the dialogue "Sursum Corda" and concludes with the final doxology; however, from the early Middle Ages this title was placed after the Sanctus.
Celebration of the Holy Communion	the sacramental meal which constitutes the second part of the Holy Eucharist in the 1979 Book of Common Prayer. Since Dom Gregory Dix, we have come to speak of it as consisting of four actions: (1) taking bread and wine; (2) giving thanks; (3) breaking the bread; and (4) sharing the bread and wine. The names customarily given to these actions are (1) the Offertory; (2) the Great Thanksgiving; (3) the Fraction; and (4) Communion, although the name Offertory for the "taking" is not strictly correct, since the bread and wine "taken" here are properly offered in the Great Thanksgiving.
Collect	a short prayer. The "collect for the day" and two other collects have traditionally concluded the Anglican office; a collect for the King or the "decalogue collect" has followed the Ten Commandments; the "collect for the day" ends the entrance rite and begins the readings; and a

194   GLOSSARY:

"postcommunion" collect follows the reception of Communion. The classical Roman rite also had an offertory collect known as the "secreta" or "super oblata;" in the 1979 Eucharist, a collect may conclude the Prayers of the People.

Communion
sharing the sacramental bread and wine. This has often given its name to the whole eucharistic rite. It was also used as the name for the psalm sung during Communion or (in 1549) the sentence of Scripture said after Communion.

Dialogue
an exchange between the officiant and the congregation. The dialogue which opens the Great Thanksgiving starts with the Salutation (sometimes omitted) and the Sursum corda.

Dismissal
the announcement, given by the deacon in historic rites, that the congregation may depart. Omitted by Cranmer at the end of the Eucharist in 1549, it was restored in the 1979 Book of Common Prayer.

Doxology
an ascription of praise to God. The Gloria in excelsis has sometimes been known as the "Greater Doxology" and the Gloria Patri as the "Lesser Doxology." The term more often refers to the concluding ascription of praise to the triune God at the end of prayers and hymns.

Epiclesis
the invocation of the Holy Spirit—in the Eucharist upon the worshiper and/or the bread and wine. In the English rite of 1549 and the Scottish rite of 1637 this came before the Institution Narrative in the Eucharistic Prayer; in Scottish rites after 1764 and American rites it follows the anamnesis or oblation.

Eucharist
Thanksgiving—the traditional name for the eucharistic prayer and—by extension—the whole rite (for which the title in the 1979 Book of Common Prayer is "The Holy Eucharist").

Eucharistic Prayer	the central prayer of the Celebration of the Holy Communion, known as "The Great Thanksgiving" in the 1979 Book of Common Prayer. Properly speaking, its full form begins with the Dialogue and concludes with the final doxology. The English rite after 1552 detached the dialogue, preface, and Sanctus from the beginning of the prayer and the portion after the Institution Narrative from the end of the prayer.
Fraction	the breaking [of the bread] at the Celebration of the Holy Communion. In classical rites this follows after the eucharistic prayer, either before or after the Lord's Prayer. The 1549 rubrics simply specified that breads be broken before distribution in Communion. The 1552 and 1559 rubrics make no mention of the fraction (which nonetheless would have been a practical necessity). Later Prayer Books called for the bread to be broken during the Institution Narrative; in the 1979 rite it was transferred to its original place. Originally a practical action (the bread was broken so that all might share) it was later given a theological interpretation (Christ's body broken for us).
Gloria in excelsis	"Glory to God in the highest"—a prose hymn used in the morning office in the Eastern Church and eventually used as a festive song of praise at the beginning of the Proclamation of the Word of God in the Western church.
Humble Access	a title for Cranmer's prayer beginning "We do not presume to come to this thy table . . ." (originally part of the Communion devotions and restored to this place in American rites after 1928; but moved in 1552 to a place immediately after the Sanctus), which articulates the reverence with which the communicant approaches the holy table for Communion.
Institution Narrative	the story of the Last Supper, incorporated into the eucharistic prayer. In the Reformed tradition,

196

however, it was not included in the eucharistic prayer but read as a warrant for the celebration.

Invocation calling the Holy Spirit upon a person or thing. See epiclesis for the use of this word to designate a part of the eucharistic prayer. It is used as a marginal title in the Scottish rite and in the American rites before 1979.

Kyrie eleison "Lord, have mercy"—a short supplication originally used as the response to the petitions of a litany. Without the petitions it came to be used in the West in a threefold, sixfold, or ninefold form at the beginning of the Eucharist and before the Lord's Prayer at the office. In 1552 Cranmer used it in an expanded form as a response to each of the ten commandments (decalogue), a Genevan custom.

Litany a series of petitions, each followed by a brief response on the part of the people. The Great Litany of the 1979 Book of Common Prayer derives from Cranmer's work before the publication of the 1549 Book of Common Prayer and was appointed to be recited after Morning Prayer on Sundays, feasts, and Wednesdays and Fridays. The 1979 rite prints two litanies based on Greek models which may be used for the Prayers of the People.

Liturgy "a public work" in its original secular meaning, it came to be applied to a service of worship as "the work of the people of God." In a narrower sense it is sometimes applied to that portion of a service designated for a certain group of persons at worship—the liturgy of the celebrant, or the deacon, or the people. It is also used to designate a historic family of rites (e.g., the Anglican liturgy) or text for the Eucharist (e.g., the Liturgy of St. Basil). In a broader sense, it is used for a form of worship that has a "fixed script" in order to facilitate everyone's participation and is contrasted to "nonliturgical worship," which uses no fixed texts.

Manual Acts

the actions of the celebrant with his hands—generally in reference to the actions of the celebrant during the eucharistic prayer, especially during the Institution Narrative.

Memorial

a term in the Scottish rite of 1637 for the portion of the eucharistic prayer after the Institution Narrative, also called in that rite the Prayer of Oblation. Presently the Greek form anamnesis is more commonly used in this regard, and the designation is limited to the first part of this portion of the eucharistic prayer, where the church declares its intention to offer the Eucharist in remembrance of Christ in accordance with his commandment at the Last Supper.

Oblation

the offering of gifts to God. This is used to describe a preliminary offering of the bread and wine when they are prepared (the "lesser oblation" which is explicitly required by the Scottish rite and by the 1928 American rite) and the offering of these gifts in the course of the eucharistic prayer (where it is a marginal title in Scottish rites after 1764 and American rites until 1979). For other uses of the word, see the definition given above in part I of this glossary.

Offertory

the first part of the Celebration of the Holy Communion when alms are collected and the bread and wine prepared. A preliminary offering of the bread and wine has sometimes been made at this time (see Oblation). Since they are properly offered in the Great Thanksgiving, in recent times many have preferred to avoid this term for this part of the service. The name is sometimes given to the sentence, psalm, hymn, or anthem used to "cover" the action during this part of the service and to the prayer sometimes used to conclude the action.

GLOSSARY:

Pascha Nostrum	"Christ our Passover [1549: Pascal lamb] is sacrificed for us"—a text found after the Lord's Prayer in the 1549 rite and adapted for use as an anthem during the breaking of the bread in the 1979 rite.
Peace	the greeting used in historic rites just before the offertory and exchanged by the congregation in the form of a kiss. The greeting was moved at an early era in the Roman rite to a place immediately before Communion, where it is found in the 1549 rite. Cranmer deleted it in 1552. In 1979 it was restored in the American rite in its original position (although it is also permitted in its 1549 position). In this rite it is used as a greeting between celebrant and congregation and may also be exchanged among members of the congregation with an appropriate gesture (commonly a handshake or embrace).
Postcommunion	the prayer or collect which follows Communion. Sometimes this term is also used for the scriptural sentence or psalm which originally "covered" the action of Communion.
Post-Sanctus	the portion of the eucharistic prayer that follows the Sanctus. In the Scottish and American rites, the link to the Sanctus has been made textually by the use of the word "glory" in the opening of this part of the prayer. In English rites after 1552 (and American rites before 1928) the Prayer of Humble Access was intruded between the Sanctus and the post-Sanctus.
Prayer for the Whole State of Christ's Church	the principal prayer of intercession in Cranmer's rite—named after the bidding which opens it. Properly it is an intercession only for the church, and not for the world. In 1549 it followed the Sanctus; in 1552 Cranmer moved it to a position after the offering of alms. Scottish Episcopalians in 1764 moved it to a position immediately after the eucharistic prayer, to which it forms the intercessory conclusion. In 1552 the words

"militant here in earth" were added to the bidding, to indicate that prayer was not offered for the departed. The original form of the bidding is used in Scottish and American rites, although in 1979 "and the world" was added in the American rite to expand the scope of the prayer. In the English rite it was rubrically included in Ante-Communion; in 1789 Americans excluded it from Ante-Communion. In Rite I of the 1979 Book of Common Prayer, it is the form of the Prayers of the People printed in the text of the Proclamation of the Word of God, although other forms may be used.

Prayer of Consecration

properly speaking, the eucharistic prayer. From the late sixteenth century, this term was used in the English rite for the portion of the prayer from the post-Sanctus to the end of the Institution Narrative and the title was incorporated into Scottish Prayer Books, the English Prayer Book of 1662, and American Prayer Books until 1979.

Prayers of the People

the intercessions after the readings and the sermon in the Proclamation of the Word of God. These prayers are also known as the "prayers of the faithful" and fell into disuse when introductory litanies became common and intercessions were also incorporated into the eucharistic prayer. Recent liturgical revisions have generally restored the Prayers of the People to their primitive place.

Preface

"the proclamation" [of the mighty acts of God]— a term originally used for the Great Thanksgiving. When the term came to be understood improperly in the sense of "introduction" it was restricted to the portion of the Great Thanksgiving which follows the opening dialogue and leads into the Sanctus. The "preface tone" is the melodic formula used as a recitative for the solemn prayers of the celebrant in Christian liturgy (including the blessing of the font and the blessing

GLOSSARY:

of the palms) and was originally used for the whole eucharistic prayer.

Proclamation of the Word of God the name given by the 1979 Book of Common Prayer to the first part of the Holy Eucharist, which consists of (1) the gathering or entrance rite, (2) the readings, sermon, and Creed, or "The Word of God," and (3) the Prayers of the People, Confession, and Peace. It is ultimately derived from the synagogue service on the Sabbath.

Reading Pew a pew used by the officiant to read the office and often the Litany and Proclamation of the Word of God from the Reformation until the Gothic Revival. It was often combined with a similar pew for the clerk, who led the responses and intoned metrical psalms and chants, and with the pulpit in a structure known as the "three-decker"—the clerk's pew being on the lowest level, the reading pew on the second, and the pulpit on the highest level.

Salutation the greeting (normally, "The Lord be with you") exchanged between the celebrant and the people at certain places in liturgical rites.

Sanctus "Holy, holy, holy Lord, God of power and might"—the hymn based on Isaiah 6 incorporated into the eucharistic prayer as a congregational song.

Sunday Morning Service the service rubrically appointed for Sunday mornings. Until 1856 in the United States and 1872 in England, this included Morning Prayer, the Litany, and Ante-Communion at all times, and also Baptism (after the second lesson of Morning Prayer) and Communion when they were celebrated. After the dates given above, Morning Prayer and Eucharist came generally to be celebrated on Sunday as separate services.

Supplication a prayer of petition. The Liturgy of Prayer Book Studies IV uses this term for the portion of the eucharistic prayer following the Invocation—a useful label for the conclusion of the prayer.

Sursum Corda

"Lift up your hearts"—the bidding (often prefaced by the Salutation) which begins the dialogue at the opening of the eucharistic prayer.

Trisagion

"Holy God, holy and mighty, holy immortal one, have mercy upon us"—a Greek prose hymn authorized in 1979 as an alternative to the Kyrie eleison at the Eucharist. In the eighteenth and nineteenth centuries, this name was often inaccurately given to the Sanctus.

APPENDIX

Schematic Architectural Plans

The following plans are meant to illustrate typical architectural settings for Anglican worship. Figures 1–7 illustrate plans related to Chapters 1 and 2; Figure 8 is a typical Gothic Revival and illustrates the "architectural revolution" spoken of in Chapter 3; Figure 9 represents one way of designing a building for worship in accordance to the 1979 Book of Common Prayer (Chapters 5 and 6).

Solid lines indicate walls or changes in elevation; double lines, screens; pews are also enclosed in solid lines. The following symbols are used in these drawings:

T	altar table	F	font
P	pulpit	R	reading pew (or desk)
C	clerk's pew (or desk)	O	organ
Sl	singers	s-s	screen
CS	clergy seats	M	musician's table (for music)
L	lectern	3	three-decker (pulpit with reading and clerk's pews

Figures 1–7 are redrawn from G. W. O. Addleshaw and Frederick Etchells, *The Architectural Setting of Anglican Worship* (London, Faber and Faber, 1948) and Dell Upton, *Holy Things and Profane* (MIT Press, Cambridge, MA, 1986). Notes on these figures tell

203

where in these books the plans are to be found, and the reader should consult these books for a detailed discussion of the buildings. Figures 8 and 9 are the work of the author.

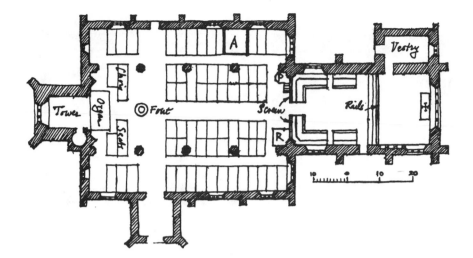

Figure 1. Burnstone, North Riding, Yorkshire. A medieval building "reseated" in 1627. Present fittings are mid-Victorian but follow the earlier arrangements. Note the chancel stalls for communicants and the singers' pews at the rear with the organ. The new Reformation use of the two rooms of a medieval church can clearly be seen in this example, where the nave is used for the Proclamation of the Word of God and the chancel for the Celebration of the Holy Communion. In the sixteenth century the altar table might have been brought down at Communion and placed lengthwise in the chancel aisle. Redrawn from Addleshaw and Etchells, Plan 3.

Schematic Architectural Plans

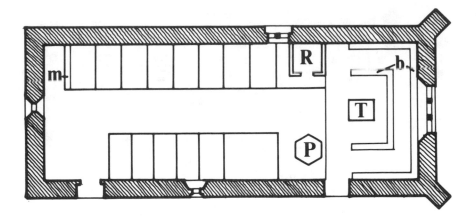

Figure 2. Langley Chapel, Shropshire, ca. 1601. There is no screen. Reading pew and pulpit are at the front on opposite sides. Note the musicians' table at the rear. Note also the communicants' benches around the altar. Redrawn from Addleshaw and Etchells, Plan 29, and Upton, Figure 40.

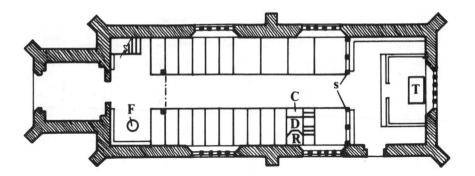

Figure 3. Foremark Church, Derbyshire, 1662. Note the screen separating off the chancel and the clerk's pew, reading pew, and pulpit on the south aisle. The font is by the entrance through the tower. A gallery over the west end might have been used for singers. Redrawn from Addleshaw and Etchells, Plan 6, and Upton, Figure 39.

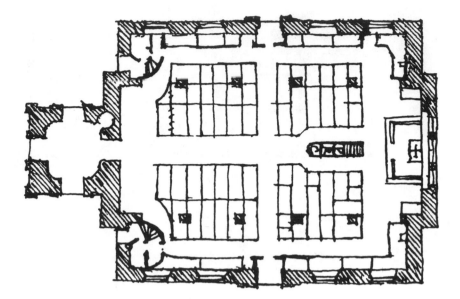

Figure 4. St. James, Picadilly, London, 1684. Note the three-decker in the central aisle. Later the pulpit was moved to one side and the reading pew and clerk's pew to the other. Organ and pulpit would have been in the gallery. This is a typical design by Sir Christopher Wren. Redrawn from Addleshaw and Etchells, Plan 10.

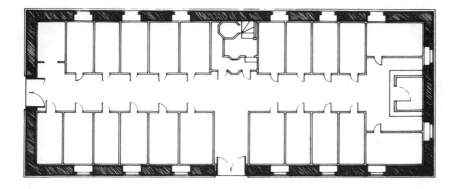

Figure 5. Middle Church, Christ Church Parish, Middlesex County, Virginia, begun 1712. Note the screen, the pulpit, and pew on the north wall. Redrawn from Upton, Figure 70.

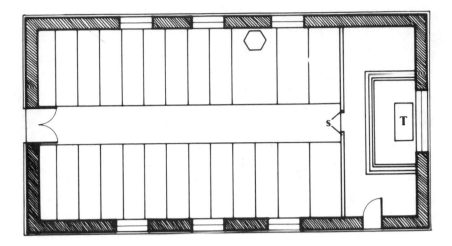

Figure 6. Little Fork Church, Culpeper County, Virginia, 1773–1776. Note the entrances at the west and south walls and the reading pew and pulpit on the north wall. Redrawn from Upton, Figure 110.

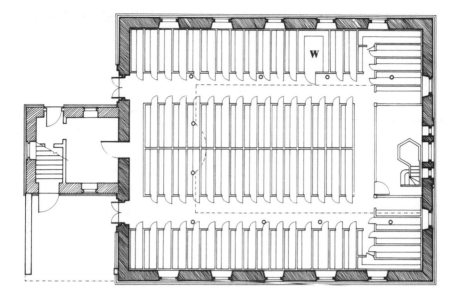

Figure 7. Christ Church, Alexandria, Virginia. Note the pulpit in front. There is no original reading pew; the clergy would perhaps have been seated in a front pew or chairs in the chancel. The altar table was below the pulpit. This is like the arrangement favored by Bishop Hobart, except that he preferred a less dominant pulpit and a more prominent altar table. Another arrangement would place the table and rails at the end opposite the reading pew and pulpit, as in St. Peter's Church, Philadelphia. Redrawn from Upton, Figure 261.

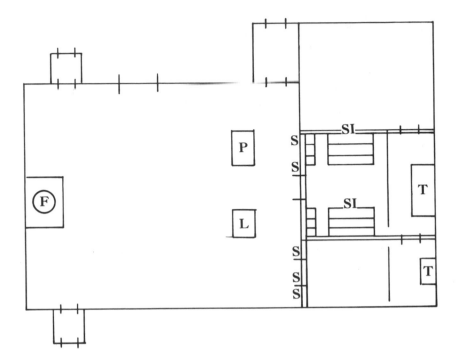

Figure 8. A Gothic Revival Plan (based loosely on Christ Church, New Haven, Connecticut). This shows a typical well-designed church in the Gothic Revival Style. The screen across the chancel is open. The chancel is raised above the level of the nave, the altar above the level of the chancel. A chapel for daily services adjoins the chancel. Less successful adaptations of the Gothic were narrower (as were medieval churches). Redesign of older churches built in other ("one-room") styles along these lines often resulted in a cramped choir and altar, for choirs had to be added onto the buildings or squeezed between the altar and the congregational seating. Seating in Christ Church, New Haven, utilizes chairs; except in cathedrals, however, slip pews were far more commonly used in Gothic Revival buildings. Sketch by the author.

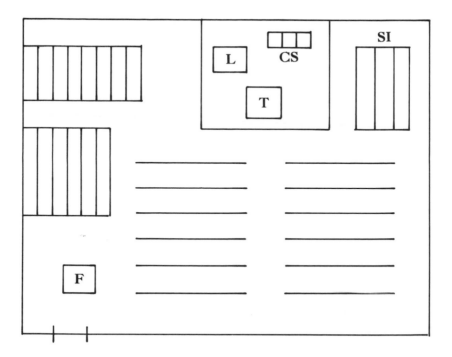

Figure 9. A contemporary configuration. This sketch shows a church with seating on three sides of the altar. The pulpit is used for both lessons and sermon. The choir is seated to the right of the altar. The font is located in its traditional place near the door. For adult baptism by partial immersion, dressing facilities would need to be provided nearby. Sketch by the author.

Index

Holy Week, 154
Hook, Walter, 85
Hooker, Richard, 14, 15, 51
Hopkins, John, 57
House of Bishops, 58, 97, 105
House of Deputies, 105
How we got where we are today,
    159–63
Humble Access, Prayer of, 4, 7, 19,
    39, 63, 66, 100, 107, 111, 140,
    150, 161
Huntington, William Reed, 98–99,
    105, 116
Hymnal (Episcopal Church; 1871),
    94, 102
Hymnal (1940), 108, 109
Hymnal 1982, The, 155, 170
Hymns Ancient and Modern, 94

Innes, Bishop George, 68
Institution Narrative, 4, 7, 35, 39,
    142, 147, 148
Institution of ministers, office for the,
    95
Interim Eucharist Sharing, 174
Introduction to Liturgical Theology
    (Schmemann), 129
Invocation, 4, 35, 39, 122, 146
    of the Spirit, 147
Irenaeus, 16

James I (England; VI of Scotland),
    10, 33
James II, 33
Jebb, John, 85
Jefferson, Thomas, 54
Jewel, Bishop John, 20–21
Jewish roots of Christian worship
    (liturgy), 126, 128
Johnson, John, 15–16, 17, 21, 22,
    37, 70

Johnson, Samuel, 15, 50, 51, 52, 69,
    70
Jones, Bayard Hale, 117, 118
Jungmann, Josef, 128
Justification by grace, doctrine of,
    92
Justin, 16

Kavanagh, Aidan, 165–66
King's Chapel, Boston, 53
Knox, John, 33, 36
Kyrie eleison, 3, 6, 7, 64, 92, 100,
    110, 112, 119, 138, 141, 143,
    173, 174

Ladd, Dean William Palmer, 116
Laity, role of, 168
Language in Worship: Reflections on a
    Crisis (Stevick), 131
Latitudinarians, 53, 54, 57, 70
Laud, Archbishop William, 10, 31,
    34, 77, 116
Laudians, 31, 86
Laud's liturgy, 34
Leeds Parish Church, 85, 88
Leo XIII, Pope, 112
Leonine prayers, 112
Lima rites, 174
Litany, 54, 55, 62, 65, 97, 100, 101,
    109, 110, 119
    Great, 141, 143, 146
Liturgical Movement, 95, 115–18,
    160, 161, 163
Liturgical Piety (Bouyer), 128
Liturgy and Society (Hebert),
    116
Liturgy for Living (Price and Weil),
    130–31
Liturgy of Church of South India
    (1950), 123, 126, 131
Liturgy of St. James, 37, 161